D1789238

VINTAGE SINGAPORE

SOUVENIRS FROM THE RECENT PAST

VINTAGE SINGAPORE

SOUVENIRS FROM THE RECENT PAST

Text by CHUNG MAY KHUEN
ONG MAY ANNE
SIM WAN HUI
TAMILSELVI SIVA
JASON TOH
WONG HONG SUEN

N M
S
National Museum
of Singapore

Editions Didier Millet

Chief Editor
Lee Chor Lin

Executive Editor
Melisa Teo

Editors
Joanna Greenfield
Hairani Hassan
Ibrahim Tahir

Text
Chung May Khuen
Ong May Anne
Sim Wan Hui
Tamilselvi Siva
Jason Toh
Wong Hong Suen

Photography
Ken Cheong Hock Cheun

Production
Sin Kam Cheong

First published in 2006 by:
Editions Didier Millet Pte Ltd
121 Telok Ayer Street, #03-01
Singapore 068590
www.edmbooks.com

and

National Museum of Singapore
93 Stamford Road
Singapore 178897
www.nationalmuseum.sg

Printed in Singapore.

© Editions Didier Millet Pte Ltd and
National Museum of Singapore.

All rights reserved. No part of this publication
may be reproduced or transmitted in any form or
by any means, electronic or mechanical, including
photocopying, recording or any information storage
and retrieval system, without the prior written
permission of the copyright owners.

ISBN 10: 981-4217-01-8
ISBN 13: 978-981-4217-01-9

Opposite: Singaporean children
clamber over a Morris Oxford
utility truck in the early 1950s.

Cover images: His Master's Voice
record, see pages 48–49; Poster
featuring Lux toilet soap, see
page 72; Cat's-eye spectacles,
see page 160; Girl brand face
powder, see page 155; Orange
telephone, see page 185. Back
cover: Suitcase, see page 142,
Shoes, see pages 146–147.

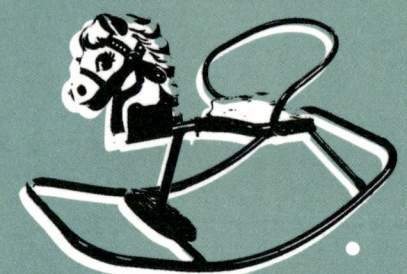

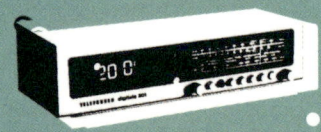

AGES
AFROM THE PAST

KEEPSAKES FROM THE PAST

Nostalgia: a sentimental yearning for a period of the past; a wistful memory of an earlier time; or a thing which evokes a former era.

Contact with objects from the past, or that are associated with the past, can evoke powerful recollections. Just by touching an old school tie, one is immediately transported to the days of assembly halls and tuck shops, of flag-raising ceremonies and recess games. We all experience nostalgia. Our capacity to remember reinvigorates our existence and defines our individuality. The personal keepsakes we treasure—the cinema ticket stub, the Squirrel savings bank, the sports trophy—are all given significance because of the memories they evoke.

Progress is a forward movement towards a goal. As we expend our energies on the future, we move away from where we were; delighting in development, yet vaguely sensing a loss. Even as things change and develop,

A group of children from the Bukit Panjang Secondary School pose in front of the National Museum during a school-trip in 1950.

This page: As Singapore gained independence from Great Britain in 1963, the Cultural Festival Show, held that year at the National Theatre, held great significance as a celebration of cultural identity.

Opposite: Before independence in 1963 and then separation in 1965, Singapore experienced turbulent times. Here students are seen demonstrating outside what was the colonial government's Assembly House in 1955. In 2004, the building re-opened as The Arts House at the Old Parliament and now plays host to various art exhibitions and concerts.

we feel the need to conserve elements of our culture so that it is not lost for future generations—or indeed for ourselves.

The National Museum of Singapore houses objects donated by (or sometimes purchased from) hundreds of individuals. Each item in the collection, much like our own personal keepsakes, connects us to the past. Seen as a whole, the collection evokes the common memory of the entire nation.

The curators of the museum have focused on the period of the 1950s to the 1970s for the Living Galleries. This was an important period in Singapore's history, not just in terms of its political development, but also culturally. Perhaps most significantly, was a thriving film industry that saw local production companies bring over 300 films to Singapore, heightening the popularity of cinema. Indeed, this 25-year period proved to be the golden age of

Singapore's film history. Similarly, fashion was pushing the boundaries and during this period women would sometimes replace their traditional dress with imported designs of Western-style clothing.

In the 1950s, Singapore was recovering from the effects of the Japanese Occupation. Politically, it was still a British colony but the seeds of decolonisation had been sown. Self-government was attained in 1959, followed by independence in 1965. By the end of 1971, and despite previous assurances that the departure would be a gradual one, the British military had completely withdrawn from Singapore, leaving it a fully independent nation.

This period was also a time of social and economic change. Trade union membership and support were strong, and the movement was politically active. Thousands would congregate to hear charismatic trade

The standard of living rose dramatically during the 1960s. As women gathered their own disposable income, department stores such as Robinsons at Raffles Place, supplied them with the goods they desired.

unionists stir the crowd. Demonstrations became frequent and there were traumatic events, such as the labour strikes and riots of the 1950s and 1960s, when some were killed in the ensuing mêlées. There were also sustained, large-scale developments such as the rapid urbanisation that physically transformed the island. The economic boom, which caused per capita GDP to rise from just over $1,300 in 1960 to nearly $9,000 by the late 1970s, resulted in radical changes and improvements in lifestyles.

Certain changes experienced during the post-World-War-II period, such as intense industrialisation and the increase in the number of women working outside the home, were not unique to Singapore. Owing to Singapore's geographical position, entrepôt economy and colonial history, external influences continued to shape the Singaporean way of life. The growth of cinema, and later television, meant that popular American and British culture made even quicker inroads into the Singaporean psyche. Naturally, these developments and influences had a huge

impact on product types and designs. With mechanisation and mass production, for instance, plastic became the material of choice for items ranging from television sets to crockery, from earrings to boots. Synthetic fabrics were mass produced, often featuring unabashedly cheerful, geometric prints that reflected the optimism and exuberance of the post-World-War-II generation. Such fabrics were popular also because they were easy to care for at a point when women had less time for laundry and ironing.

Style and Revival
From home furnishings to hairstyles, twenty-first-century designers are constantly re-interpreting and incorporating elements from products of the post-World-War-II period or copying them completely. What has commonly been described as 'retro' fashion has been adopted by trendsetters the world over. Current high-tech stereo systems are being clad in vintage radio casings, and iconic cars such as the Mini have been re-launched. One might dismiss this as the usual designer habit

of seeking inspiration from the past. It is more likely, however, that this fascination with 'retro' style stems from the nostalgic pangs of the post-World-War-II 'baby boomer' generation. Having experienced immense change at a time when traditions were constantly being challenged, the reminiscence of this generation is particularly strong.

Interesting and collectable artefacts from this period are readily available and can be found in flea markets and forgotten corners of closets. What has hitherto been lacking, however, is an attempt to assemble a coherent collection that is accompanied by a detailed explanation in the context of Singapore's social history. The National Museum of Singapore aims to do just that.

The artefacts in the collection, which can be seen in this book, serve as potent reminders to those who lived through these pivotal years, and they help to illustrate the realities of life in Singapore's recent past to those who were born later.

Themes in the Book

The purpose of *Vintage Singapore* is to showcase selected artefacts from the museum's collection, while providing a historical context in which to appreciate them. To this end, the book is divided into five thematic chapters.

Chapter One, Singapore Scene, delves into the Singaporean nightlife. It examines popular leisure activities of the period including cinema, music and dance. With the arrival of the various amusement parks that housed not only cinemas but also venues for cabarets and dances, the nature of mass-entertainment changed dramatically. Singapore was quick to absorb Western trends and local pop music was unmistakably influenced by both American and British music.

Chapter Two, Singapore Dining, examines the social significance of food. Owing to the fact that various ethnic groups intermingled freely at coffee shops and hawker stalls across Singapore, these humble eateries had a deeply

All kinds, both rich and poor, of different ethnic backgrounds frequented coffee shops, such as this one in Chinatown.

Not yet accustomed to the comforts of air-conditioning, on particularly warm days, those living near a pond, river or sea had no qualms about jumping in.

unifying effect. This was in stark contrast to hotel dining rooms and social clubs, which—by virtue of their high prices—excluded most local Singaporeans.

Chapter Three, Singapore Childhood, is devoted to the younger generation of the 1950s–1970s period. A typical day for a child of school age meant attending school and then helping out with chores, babysitting younger siblings, and playing in or around the home. Private tuition was virtually unheard of until the 1970s, although organised extra-curricular activities, including the Scouts and Brownies, already existed. For the most part children amused themselves, playing games that were low on technology but high on improvisation or physical activity, such as five stones, *catching* (tag) and marbles. Much playtime was spent outdoors because homes were small or simply too unappealing to spend time in.

Chapter Four, Singapore Style, is about the fashion of the period. As with other aspects of life in Singapore, Western styles sat comfortably against an Asian backdrop. As fashion was most obviously reflected in

what women wore, this chapter also examines the significance of women to family and society. Between 1950 and 1979, the number of women employed outside the home surged as girls received better education and as Singapore became more industrialised. Women's roles shifted in tandem with changes in the economy and society.

Chapter 5, Singapore Home, traces the improvements experienced in living conditions from the 1950s to the 1970s. From the end of World War II to the late 1950s, much of the population lived in shop houses, in which the upper levels were often partitioned into small living quarters. Many people had to tolerate crowded conditions. Sanitation was poor and residents were forced to share communal kitchen and bathroom facilities. This began to change with the formation of the Housing & Development Board (HDB), in February 1960. Adopting the first statutory Master Plan for the urbanisation of Singapore, formulated in 1958, the HDB's ambitious building programme provided Singaporeans with brand-new, clean and comfortable homes.

The Housing & Development Board (HDB) was established in 1960. These HDB flats, pictured in 1962, are in Kallang.

As families moved away from shop houses and *kampongs* into their new HDB flats they also aspired to modern home appliances such as refrigerators and washing machines. However, certain trade-offs were unavoidable. For those who had lived in the *kampongs* there was a sense that the familiar spirit of *gotong royong* (mutual care) had been lost.

Window to the Past

In modern Singapore, barely recognisable compared with what it was twenty years ago, our pangs of nostalgia persist. Furthermore, our appreciation of all things that have passed lends an understanding of the present. Indeed as we learn from the past, the contact with the carefully gathered artefacts featured in this book makes our understanding all the more poignant. The museum's collection represents the best of the period and the artefacts are of enduring interest and importance—the collection shows a *Vintage Singapore* we are eager to remember.

This page: Guests dressed to the nines in modified Asian and Western-style attire enjoy a birthday party.

Opposite: The happy days of childhood; schoolgirls pose for their picture.

This page from top: Chinese women enjoying a day out in the park; an important means of transport, bus companies suffered from operational difficulties and labour unrest before their reorganisation in the early 1970s; a coffee shop in Serangoon Road.

Opposite from top: A Chinese coffee shop in 1962; women shop at a goldsmiths; a mother and her children at home.

SINGAPORE SCENE

While the nation shrugged off the restraints of war, revellers enjoyed the amusement parks and cinemas where live shows, dances and film showed them a good time.

As the urban population of Singapore grew, more commercial and Western-influenced concepts of entertainment began to emerge. In the 1920s and 1930s, the amusement park and cinema arrived on the Singapore scene, offering a range of fashionable leisure experiences. Here, film, music and dance all contributed to a vibrant, some say glamorous, nightlife.

Great World Amusement Park at Kim Seng Road, New World at Kitchener Road, and Happy World (later renamed Gay World) in Geylang, provided affordable mass entertainment during their 1920s–1950s heyday. Amid the carnival atmosphere, the parks offered various recreational choices, from sporting events to cabarets held in music halls, from popular theatre to cinema. During the 1920s, fairground cinemas were a novel attraction, and the arrival of talkies (film with sound) increased the popularity of cinema-going even further. American films were the most

Guests at the Singapore Civil Service New Year Dinner and Dance enjoy a cabaret show at the Neptune Theatre Restaurant in January 1979.

popular, followed by British and Chinese films. Additionally, Hindi films were enjoyed by Singapore's Malay and Indian audience.

Before the advent of television broadcasts in 1963, cinema remained the main form of visual entertainment for Singaporeans. Patrons were prepared to queue for hours for tickets and the resulting black market led some cinemas to limit each person to four tickets. Prices, which ranged from $1 to $3, barely changed between the 1950s and the 1970s, making cinema tickets relatively more affordable as time passed.

Among the theatres to choose from were Cathay, one of the first cinemas to resume business after the war; Capitol, which in 1952 became one of the first to screen a full-length 3D movie (*Bwana Devil*) requiring special glasses; Metropole; Rex; Odeon and many others. In the 1970s, Asia's largest drive-in cinema at Jurong could accommodate 900 vehicles. Many cinemas in those days were equipped for live entertainment such as magic shows, beauty

The old Capitol Theatre, which was bought by Shaw Brothers in 1946. It was one of the main cinemas in Singapore and exhibited all the major Hollywood blockbuster productions such as *Bwana Devil*.

The New World Amusement
Park, at Kitchener Road, was
a favourite of families, offering
entertainment to suit all tastes.

contests, dance revues, musical and variety shows
and even ice-skating events—the first of which was
staged at the Capitol in 1951.

The popularity of cinema encouraged the
growth of film exhibition and production activities
in Singapore. Disrupted by war and the Japanese
Occupation from 1942 to 1945, the cinema business
prospered soon after as the public turned to
entertainment for relief from post-war struggles.

By the late 1950s, there were two major
production companies, the Malay Film Productions
under Shaw Brothers, and Cathay–Keris Films,
a partnership between producer Ho Ah Loke and
Loke Wan Tho, the owner of Cathay Organisation.
Producing mainly Malay films, the two studios
alone made over 260 films in the 1950s and 1960s;
contributing to the most productive period in
Singapore's filmmaking history.

In the museum's collection, film star cards,
cinema tickets, film posters and other memorabilia
reflect the appeal of cinema in general. The local
entertainment magazines in the collection show the
popularity of home-grown films. These films gave
new life to love stories, epic adventures and local
legends. They were also enjoyed by many for their
musical scores and choreography.

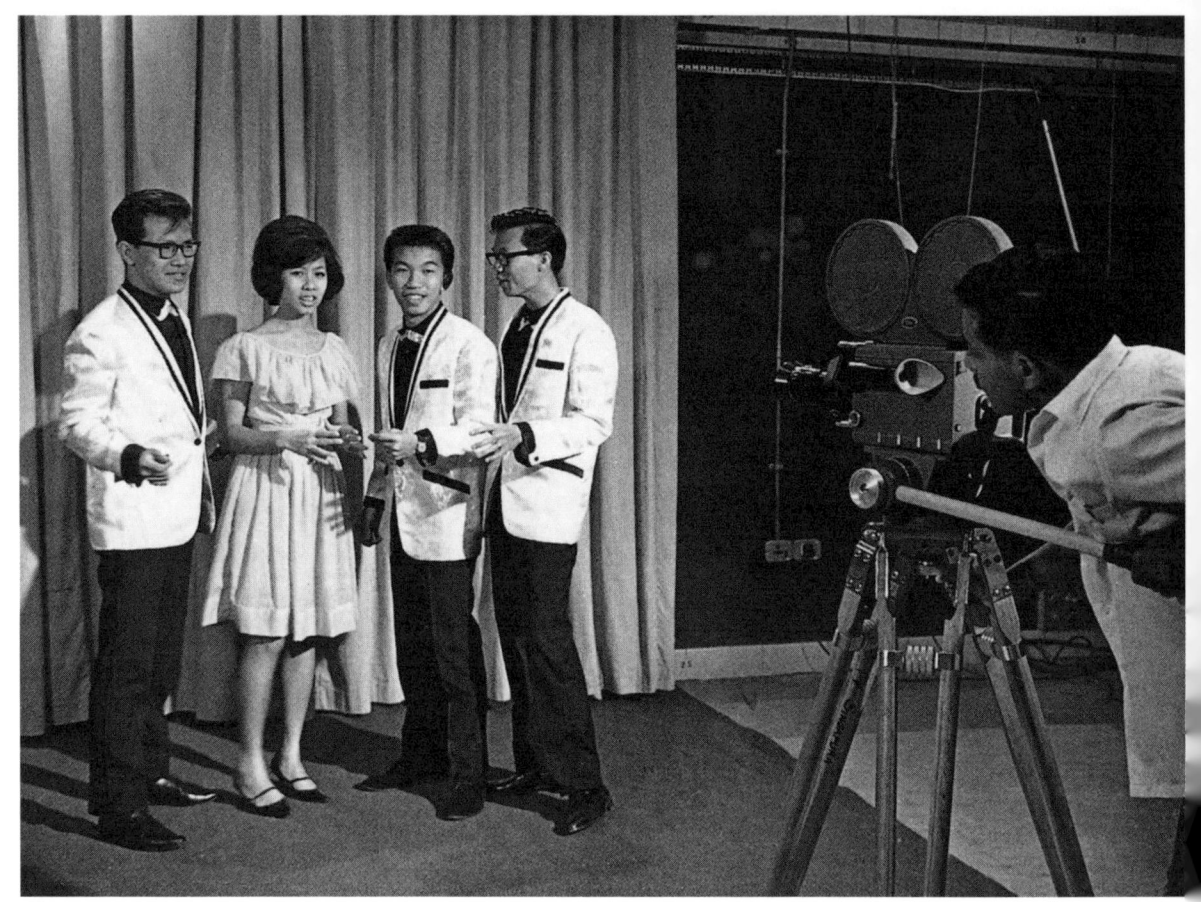

As Singapore moved towards independence and away from British rule, local film became a popular means to reflect the urban reality and social expectations. One such film was Malay Film Productions' *Penarek Becha* (Trishaw-Puller), a story about a poor trishaw-puller who falls in love with a rich young lady. The tribulations faced by the lovers reflect the disparity between the economic and social classes in the 1950s, a theme that would recur in the director P. Ramlee's subsequent features. Although relatively few Chinese-language films were produced in Singapore, a notable release was Cathay-Keris Films' first Mandarin release, *Shi Zi Cheng* (Lion City) in 1960. A love story involving the son of a factory owner and one of the firm's female rubber packers, *Shi Zi Cheng*, like *Penarek Becha*, touched on the issue of social and economic division. The publicity posters for both these films and others are included in the museum's collection.

The local studios published entertainment magazines to promote their movies and film stars. Daily newspaper advertisements, freestanding displays and hand-painted posters were all part of the aggressive promotional effort. Trucks with

This page: Local musical acts would emulate Western bands but sing in their native tongue.

Opposite: Party-goers on the dance floor doing the 'twist' during a Goodwill Committee Dinner and Dance in the Queenstown constituency, in August 1964.

large billboards were driven all over the island to announce upcoming attractions and to distribute handbills. Some of these promotional materials are part of the collection, for example, the film star cards that were distributed as gifts to boost the sale of consumer products such as bubble gum. The images of these stars were also used to endorse lifestyle goods including jewellery and soft drinks.

Besides film-related items, the museum's vinyl collection reflects the changing tastes of the audience. The collection contains vinyl records that fall into two categories: long playing discs (LPs) or albums and smaller 45 rpm discs (45's) for individual songs or singles. The local music scene was awash with homegrown acts and bands performed in various languages, sometimes switching from one language to another; for example, some sang Mandarin renditions of English songs, others sang in Malay. While some compositions utilised local traditional and folk elements, others absorbed influences from fashionable Western genres such as the cha-cha, samba, rock and roll, and the twist. The museum's collection is evidence of the multi-ethnic world of entertainment that embodied the Singapore Scene.

This page from top: Great World Amusement Park; the Cathay cinema building; merchant navy crewmembers enjoying a night out in a local bar during shore leave in 1954.

Opposite from top: The old Roxy Theatre at East Coast Road; the Odeon at North Bridge Road; a view of The Jubilee Theatre along North Bridge Road.

28. AUDREY HEPBURN

3. ROCK HUDSON

30. ELIZABETH TAYLOR

PRINTED IN HOLLAND

KIRK DOUGLAS 19
Paramount Pict.

20. MARILIN MONROE

21. MARLON BRANDO

PRINTED IN HOLLAND

LORETTA YOUNG
Metro Goldwyn-Mayer 92

96. ERROL FLYNN

DORIS DAY
W.B. 1

LINDA DARNELL
Fox.   115

ESTHER WILLIAMS
Metro Goldwyn-Mayer   83

6. JANE RUSSELL

23. RANDOLPH SCOTT

IRENE DUNNE
Fox   123

COLEEN GRAY
M.G.M   147

Hollywood films were extremely popular in Singapore, so much so that they accounted for 70 per cent of films shown in the late 1930s. The rest were British, Chinese and Indian films. In the 1950s and 1960s, film star photos were distributed as gifts to boost the sale of entertainment publications and consumer products such as bubble gum.

Film star cards, Holland,
1950s to 1960s
Card
H 5.7–7 cm x W 3.8–5.7 cm

First row from left; Audrey Hepburn 1995-05446, Rock Hudson 1995-05448, Elizabeth Taylor 1995-05449, Linda Darnell 1995-05428, Esther Williams 1995-05424, and Jane Russell 1995-05453.
Second row from left; Kirk Douglas 1995-05435, Marilyn Monroe 1995-05457, Marlon Brando 1995-05451, Randolph Scott 1995-05458, Irene Dunne 1995-05425, and Coleen Gray 1995-05430.
Third row from left; Loretta Young 1995-05431, Errol Flynn 1995-05456, and Doris Day 1995-05421.

Film star cards also depicted Asian stars. This reflects the period from the 1960s, when some Singaporean studios produced Chinese films in Hong Kong. Cathay established MP & GI Film Co. Ltd. in 1956 and Shaw Brothers built a multi-million dollar studio in Hong Kong's Clearwater Bay. Another Singapore-backed company, Guangyi Film Production, became a leading producer of Cantonese films.

Film star cards, Hong Kong, 1960s
Card
H 8.9 cm x W 6.3 cm
This page, clockwise from top left; Ge Lan 1995-05463, Le Di 1995-05464, Ye Feng 1995-05477, and You Min 1995-05479.
Opposite, first row from left; Ding Ning 1995-05470, Bai Lu Ming 1995-05478, and Ding Ning 1995-05468.

Second row from left; Du Juan 1995-05462, Lin Feng 1995-05467, Ou Jia Hui 1995-05466, and Ding Lan 1995-05474.
Third row from left; Fan Li 1995-05469, Zhong Qing 1995-05473, and Lin Feng 1995-05465.
Fourth row from left; Zhang Zhong Wen 1995-05472, Ding Hong 1995-05471, Feng Bao Bao 1995-05476, and Bai Lu Ming 1995-05475

1

In a similar trend to the film star cards, Singaporeans would also collect greeting cards featuring portraits of their friends or loved ones. Photo studios would print these cards with graphic designs and generic greetings alongside the sender's photograph. Often, the choice of the accompanying design reflected the personality of the sender, who would pen personal greetings on the back of the card.

1 Half portraits of young ladies,
Late 1960s to 1970
Gelatin prints
H 9 cm x W 7 cm
Donated by Angie Chua
2004-00829, 2004-00831, 2004-00833,
2004-00830, 2004-00832

2 Half portraits of young men, 1960s
Gelatin prints
H 8 cm x W 7 cm
2000-03733-731, 2000-03733-665,
2000-03733-681

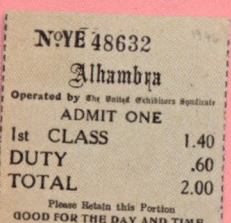

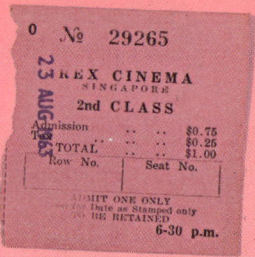

Besides film exhibition, the Shaw and Cathay Organisations also ventured into filmmaking. The two companies were the key producers of Malay films in the 1950s. These were exhibited through their respective cinema chains in Singapore and across the region.

1   Cinema tickets, 1940s to 1960s
    Paper
    H 6–11.3 cm x W 6–10.9 cm
    2001-03951, 1995-00212, 1995-05488,
    1995-05484, 2001-03952,
    1995-05490, 2001-03948

2   Glass slide, 1960s to 1970s
    Glass/polyester-based film
    H 8.2 cm x W 10 cm
    Donated by the Hollywood Theatre
    1995-01874

3   *Berdosa* film poster, 1951
    Paper
    H 76.6 cm x W 54.9 cm
    1996-00654

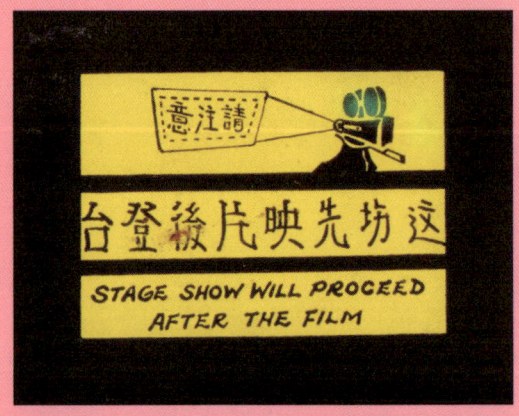

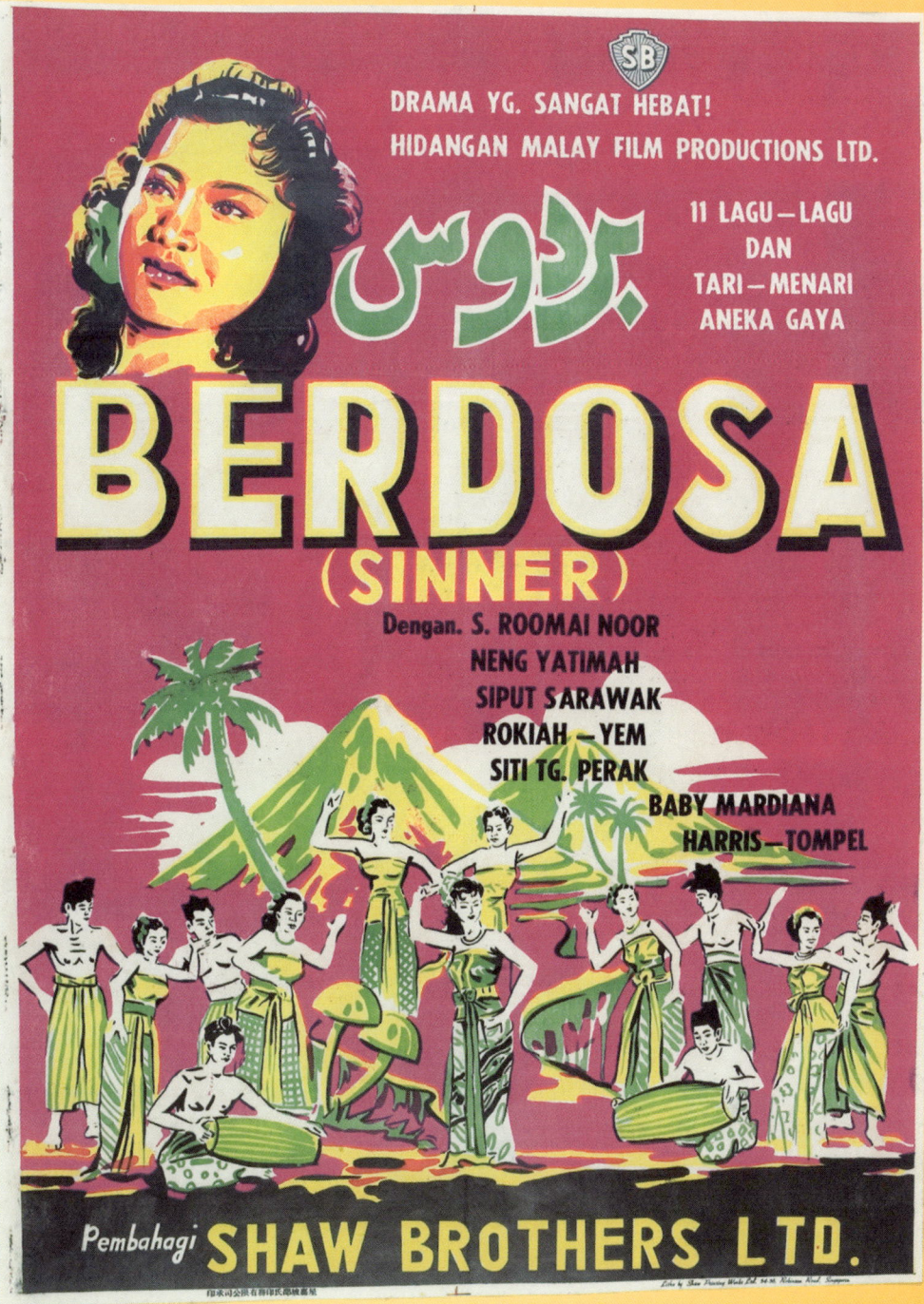

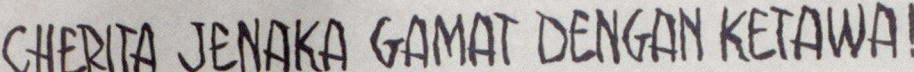

2

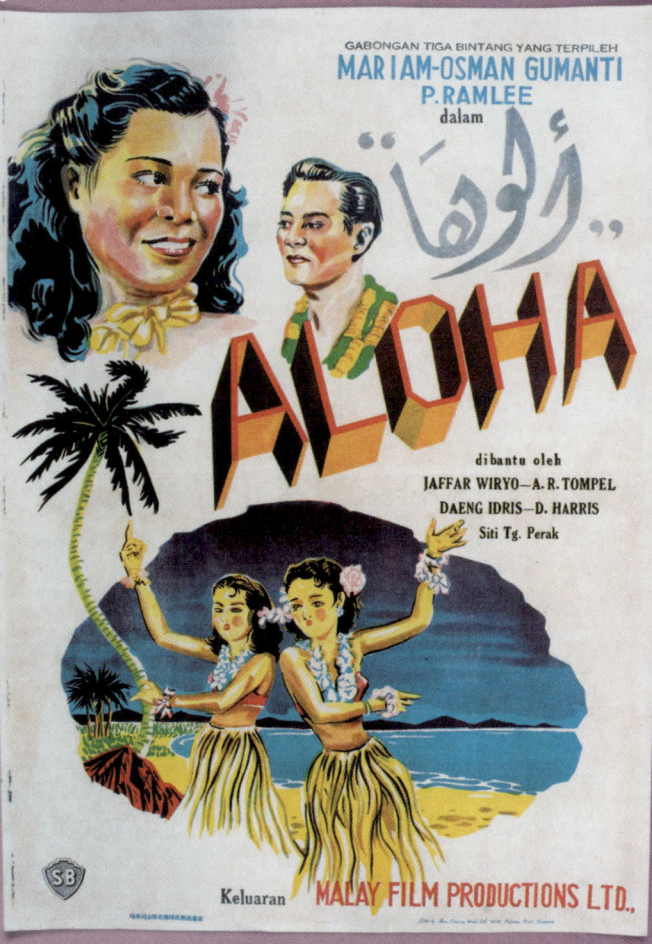

P. Ramlee was the biggest star during the Malay film industry's heyday of the 1950s and 1960s. In 1948, he came to Singapore aged 19, and over 25 years acted in 62 films, directing 33. His films ranged from historical epic and romance to social drama, comedy and horror. His directorial debut, *Penarek Becha* (1955) was a forerunner in social commentary on Malay society. His film *Bujang Lapok* (1957), based on three happy-go-lucky bachelors, created a winning comedic formula. This was followed by three sequels, *Pendekar Bujang Lapok* (1959), *Ali Baba Bujang Lapok* (1961) and *Seniman Bujang Lapok* (1961). *Pendekar Bujang Lapok* was awarded Best Comedy at the Asian Film Festival 1959 in Kuala Lumpur.

1   *Pendekar Bujang Lapok* film poster, 1959
Paper
H 79.5 cm x W 55.2 cm
1996-00653

2   *Aloha* film poster, 1950
Paper
H 79 cm x W 54.9 cm
1996-00652

3   *Penarek Becha* handbill, 1955
Paper
H 39.6 cm x W 27.3 cm
1999-00890

3

1

When Singapore was granted self-governance by the British colonial government in 1959, Cathay–Keris announced that the studio would produce Chinese-language feature films to aid the development of an independent culture for Singapore. In 1960, the studio screened its first Mandarin film, *Lion City*, a love story set against the backdrop of social class struggles and Singapore's first election.

● 1   *Lion City* film poster, 1960
       Paper
       H 37.8–39 cm x W 12.6–13.5 cm
       1997-00713

● 2   *Lion City*, film magazine cover
       featuring Miss Orchid, 1960
       Paper
       H 19 cm x W 13.5 cm
       1995-02317

To promote their films and increase popularity, actors and actresses were required to participate in promotional work and make media appearances, which were arranged by the film studios.

● 3   *Majalah Bintang*, magazine cover
       featuring Rusini, 1953
       Paper
       H 26.2 cm x W 19.6 cm
       2001-04896

● 4   *Film Raya*, magazine cover featuring
       Maria Menado, 1953
       Paper
       H 26.5 cm x W 19 cm
       2001-04979

● 5   *Majalah Bintang*, magazine cover
       featuring S. Roomai Noor and Ummi
       Kalthoum, 1956
       Paper
       H 26.2 cm x W 19.1 cm
       2001-04903

● 6   *Majalah Bintang*, magazine cover
       featuring Hashimah Yon, 1958
       Paper
       H 26.1 cm x W 18.3 cm
       2001-04911

2

Apart from film, music was a popular pastime in Singapore. Gramophone and Typewriter Ltd—later known as His Master's Voice, or HMV—from London, England and Beka Records from Germany made recording expeditions to Malaya as early as the 1900s.

● 1   His Master's Voice records,
       1950 to 1960s
       Vinyl
       Sleeve, H 26 cm x W 25.7 cm
       Record, Diam. 30 cm
       XXXX-08180-01, 1996-00812-13,
       2000-01112-01, 2000-01088

● 2   His Master's Voice advertising
       signboard, 1950s to 1970s
       Enamel
       H 45.8 cm x W 61.4 cm
       2000-03543

SINGAPORE DINING

The plethora of choice and the increasingly social character of eating out made food a pleasure rather than mere fuel, becoming a deeply entrenched Singaporean passion.

The history of street food in Singapore dates back to the nineteenth century. As late as the 1860s, the male-female ratio in Singapore was about ten to one. Male immigrants, without their female relatives to cook for them, had to rely on coffee shops and food stalls for their daily meals. It was only from the late 1940s—after the gender ratio evened out, and more people began to marry and start families—that home-cooked meals began to replace food bought from outside. Since then, food and eating have been transformed into a national passion and today street food is found not only in hawker centres, coffee shops (*kopitiam*) and food courts, but also in restaurants and hotels.

During the 1930s, Hainanese-owned coffee shops were male-dominated places where Chinese men would congregate to eat breakfast. The menu was simple: toast, eggs and coffee or tea. The coffee shops gradually became an important element in the social landscape of Singapore and

A Chinese coffee shop in Chinatown, with songbirds to accompany the customers' conversation.

by the 1950s, they had become popular places in which to meet friends and business associates. Coffee shops also started to serve food such as noodles and chicken rice porridge (*congee*), and formerly itinerant hawkers began to set up permanent stalls in the streets. Soft drink consumption also increased and companies such as Pepsi Cola and local brand Fraser and Neave experienced rapid growth.

Coffee and tea were served in thick porcelain cups and saucers and the drinks were commonly sweetened with condensed milk or sugar. As their coffee or tea was served piping hot, it was common for patrons to cool their beverage by pouring it into the saucer before drinking.

The study of street food and coffee shops provides a unique perspective on Singaporean life. Even though most experienced a relatively low standard of living in the immediate post-World-War-II decades, the vibrant interactions in the streets and the marketplace reveal an extraordinary resilience and openness.

This page: Coffee shops were owned mainly by the Hainanese. Previously, as cooks in colonial British households, the Hainanese had learnt the art of brewing coffee, filtering it through a cloth strainer before serving it in sturdy cups and saucers.

Opposite: Besides coffee shops, street stalls were popular eating places in the 1950s. These open-air, makeshift stalls could be found downtown, for example at Koek Road, Hong Kong Street and Bugis Street.

The museum's collection of food-related artefacts evolved with the museum's identity. The early food-related collection comprised wooden coconut-graters, granite pestle and mortar sets, and bamboo or rattan, basketwork. This formed part of the ethnographic collection in the early twentieth century—when the National Museum was still known as the Raffles Museum and Library—and was acquired mainly during fieldtrips carried out by curators, anthropologists and zoologists. After Singapore's independence, the museum started to collect objects of everyday life in Singapore itself, in order to document the nation's socioeconomic history.

Food-related objects make it into the collection largely incidentally. This is due to the fact that such objects are rarely kept, not even for sentimental reasons. Consequently, few donations of food-related objects are received. However, over the years, the collection has gradually grown and now includes a broad range of objects including kitchen implements, tea canisters, cookbooks, recipes, cookware and food advertising ephemera.

A significant part of the collection is related to the coffee shop. Apart from furniture, which includes a distinct L-shaped counter with

This page: Cigarettes and cookies could be bought over the counter.

Opposite: The majority of people who ate out on a regular basis were men eating alone. Some were male immigrants whose female relatives had stayed behind in their home country, others were workers who ate their lunch at street stalls and coffee shops rather than making the trip home for a hot meal.

balustrades, marble-topped round tables, and bentwood chairs, the museum has an extensive collection of coffee-shop paraphernalia. The extensive collection of cup-and-saucer-sets dates from the 1940s–1980s. Commonly featuring floral motifs, they were produced in Singapore for the export market. There are rarer samples—those that bear the product trademarks and logos that date from the early 1940s. These were distributed throughout Singapore, peninsular Malaysia and Indonesia. The cups and saucers are not only testament to product and consumption history in the post-World-War-II era of industrialisation and modern consumerism, they are also a visual documentation of design history. They show the subtle lithographic details and colours that gradually gave way to the stark and bold colours of modern advertising.

The popularity of coffee shops made them prime sites for advertisements. The advertising ephemera in the collection include trays and aluminium wall-mounted advertisements, soft drink bottles and glasses. In the 1950s, as photorealism became a worldwide trend, advertisements would often feature glamorous movie stars or well-known celebrities. However,

Calendars were used to advertise various products around the coffee shops and restaurants. Part of the museum's collection, examples of these calendars can be found on pages 74–77.

the tobacco industry was at the forefront of modern advertising and was among the first to instil brand identification and loyalty in customers.

The collection also includes a *kueh tutu* (steamed rice flour cakes) trishaw cart, a brass water boiler-cum-coffee or tea maker belonging to a *sarabat* (tea with milk and spices) stall, *ice kachang* (ice dessert) makers, hawker licences, and hawker tools and implements such as a charcoal stove, bamboo noodle strainers and brass ladles. The extensive collection of traditional cake and cookie moulds, that are carved with decorative and symbolic motifs, provide insights to the people that used them.

Household items such as tiffin carriers, cooking pots (see pages 176–177 and 180–181), and woks are also part of the food-related collection. Although the style is largely unchanged today, their material shows changes in lifestyle. For example, the shape of the basic ladle has remained the same, but its material ranges from coconut husk to plastic. Similarly, the stainless steel saucepans increasingly favoured by the middle class in the 1960s gradually replaced their earthenware counterparts.

The featured collection concentrates on the coffee-shop-related artefacts, which highlight the social role of food in Singapore.

Roadside hawker stalls
provided a place for gossip
and exchange of information.
This page from top: A hawker
stall at Collyer Quay in 1963; a
night scene; Bugis Street in 1962.

Opposite from top: Sago Lane
in 1955; street food along the
Singapore River in 1970.

● 4

Before the 1940s, coffee was sold by itinerant hawkers who congregated at the harbour, on street corners or at commercial areas to cater to workers. After the war, as the hawkers began to move into coffee shops, tea and coffee remained the standard order of customers. The new, more comfortable environment meant people could sit and linger over their drink while listening to the Rediffusion set or socialising with other customers. The brewer, usually the coffee shop owner, would expertly mix boiled water with concentrated coffee or tea. Ground coffee powder or tea dust were filtered with cotton cloth strainers. Then sugar or condensed milk were added according to taste.

● 1   Water kettle, 1970s
       Brass
       H 13 cm x W 20 cm x D 12 cm
       2006-01616

● 2   Tea kettle, 1970s
       Brass
       H 17.9 cm x W 33.9 cm x D 17.9 cm
       2006-01614

● 3   Coffee kettle, 1970s
       Brass
       H 16 cm x W 14.5 cm x D 15.6 cm
       2006-01615

● 4   Coffee kettle, 1970s
       Brass
       H 26.2 cm x W 38.6 cm x D 16.7 cm
       2006-01613

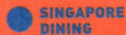 
Coffee shops would serve coffee and tea in thick porcelain cups and saucers that were stored on wooden shelves. In the 1960s, a cup of black coffee cost about 10 cents; 15 cents with milk. The cups and saucers were emblazoned with either floral motifs or the logos of the beverage companies, designed to capture the attention of the consumer.

1   Lifeguard condensed milk cup and saucer, 1970s
Porcelain
H 7.8 cm x Diam. 14.6 cm
2006-01474, 2006-01536

2   Milo cup and saucer, 1980s
Porcelain
H 7.8 cm x Diam. 14.4 cm
2006-01476, 2006-01538

3   Nescafe cup and saucer, 1970s
Porcelain
H 7.4 cm x Diam. 14.4 cm
2006-01484, 2006-01546

4   Teh Ceylon Chap Gajah cup and saucer, 1970s
Porcelain
H 8 cm x Diam. 14.8 cm
2006-01515, 2006-01577

5   Swan Tea cup and saucer, 1980s
Porcelain
H 8.1 cm x Diam. 14.9 cm
2006-01497, 2006-01559

6   Pure Creamery Butter cup and saucer, 1970s
Porcelain
H 7.4 cm x Diam. 15.2 cm
2006-01494, 2006-01556

7   Alpine Condensed Milk cup and saucer, 1960s
Porcelain
H 7.9 cm x Diam. 14.5 cm
2006-01513, 2006-01575

● 4

Cups and saucers supplied by the coffee or tea merchants, or condensed milk companies, were used to advertise their products. There were foreign and local brands, for example, Milo and Nescafe—both Nestle brands created in the 1930s in Australia and Switzerland respectively—which became very popular in Malaysia and Singapore from the 1950s. Local tea merchants and coffee shops like 555 Ribbon Tea and Aw Ah Coffee Shop also produced their own cups and saucers. In some cases, companies even printed their telephone number on the saucers.

● 1 555 Ribbon Tea cup and saucer, 1980s
Porcelain
H 7.8 cm x Diam. 14.9 cm
2006-01486, 2006-01548

● 2 888 Tea and Coffee cup and saucer, 1980s
Porcelain
H 7.8 cm x Diam. 15.1 cm
2006-01469, 2006-01531

● 3 Aw Ah Coffee Shop cup and saucer, 1980s
Porcelain
H 7.9 cm x Diam. 14.7 cm
2006-01472, 2006-01534

● 4 Cup and saucer sets, 1970s to 1980s
Porcelain
H 2.3–8.2 cm x Diam. 14.1–15 cm
2006-01482, 2006-01544, 2006-01499, 2006-01561, 2006-01526, 2006-01588

1

KHONG GUAN BISCUIT FACTORY (S) LTD.

1 Before World War II, it was mainly British officers and their families who could afford to snack on cookies. After the war however, Khong Guan Biscuits was formed and produced biscuits for the local population. During the 1950s and 1960s it established itself as having the most popular brand of biscuits. Favourites were the sultana biscuits and cream crackers.

Khong Guan biscuit container, 1950s
Tin
H 21 cm x Diam. 17 cm
1997-02204

Ovaltine was the preferred brand of energy drink in the late 1940s and 1950s. Though it was produced as a nourishing drink for children, it was also supplied to the troops during the World Wars. People in Singapore who believed in the restorative powers of Ovaltine would visit new mothers with a tin of Ovaltine and some cream crackers. Ovaltine was also a favourite suppertime drink consumed by the whole family at home and in coffee shops.

2 Ovaltine container, 1950s
Tin
H 24 cm x Diam. 12 cm
2000-06916

3 Ovaltine container, 1950s
Tin
H 19.5 cm x Diam. 14.5cm
1995-04391-001

4 Ovaltine tray, 1950s
Tin
H 27.8 cm x W 34.7 cm x D 2.5 cm
2000-03614

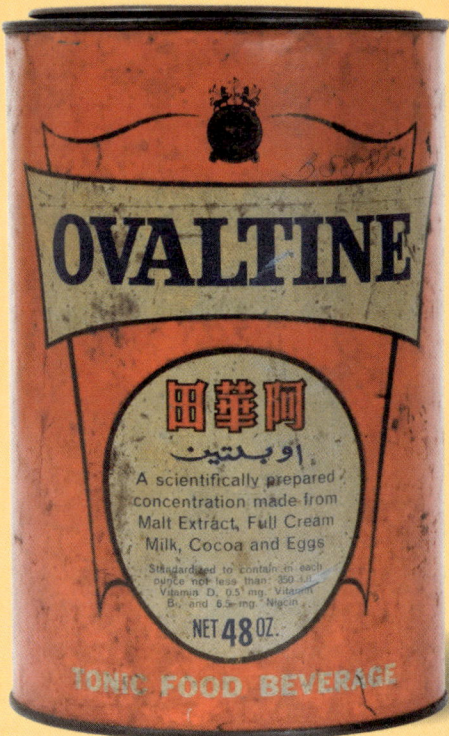

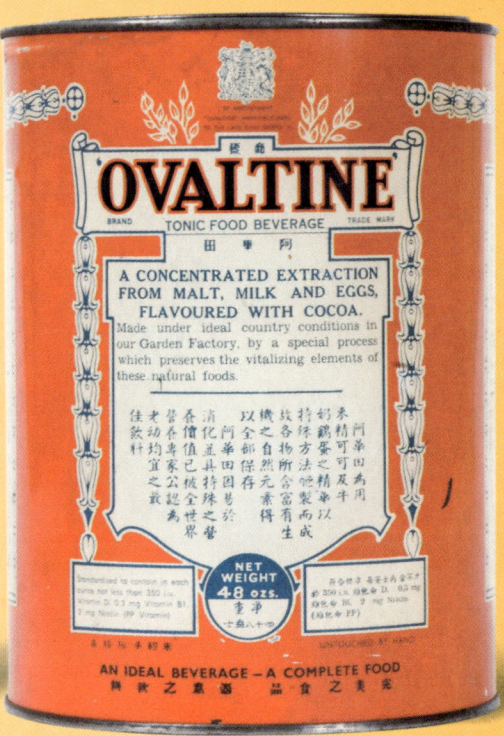

• 4

Beers! Cheers!

Time for a
Tiger

In coffee shops across Singapore, beer companies have always marketed themselves very aggressively. Beer-related paraphernalia—everything from calendars with scantily clad poster girls to ashtrays, serving trays and beer mugs—was commonly seen in coffee shops across Singapore. Selected brands of liquor, such as Johnny Walker, were also available at coffee shops.

• 1 Heineken Beer advertisement tray, 1950s
Tin
Diam. 29.3 cm x D 2.8 cm
2000-03608

• 2 Anchor Beer advertisement tray, 1950s
Tin
Diam. 31.7 cm x D 2 cm
2000-03624

• 3 Carlsberg Beer advertisement tray, 1950s
Tin
Diam. 33 cm x D 1.8 cm
2000-03613

• 4 Tiger Beer advertisement tray, 1970s
Tin
Diam. 30.1 cm x D 2.5 cm
2000-03609

• 5 White Horse Scotch Whiskey advertisement tray, 1950s
Tin
H 30.8 cm x W 30.8 cm
2000-03602

• 5

The White Horse Cellar

Estab. 1742

WHITE HORSE

Fine Old
Scotch Whisky

1

Coffee shops were so popular in the 1950s and 1960s that wealthier retailers decided to advertise their products on posters and trays. Often, popular actresses or models of the period graced these advertisements to tempt customers into spending more.

1   Poster featuring advertisement for Lux toilet soap, 1940s
Paper
H 18.9 cm x W 25.7 cm
2000-06614

2   Tray featuring advertisement for soft drinks by F & N, 1960s
Iron and print
Diam. 32 cm x D 1.5 cm
2000-03615

3   Tray featuring advertisement for Mee Kong Chai Watches Department, 1960s
Iron and print
H 25.2 cm x W 32.3 cm x D 1.8 cm
2000-03596

4   Tray featuring advertisement for Poh Heng Goldsmiths Ltd., 1960s
Iron and print
H 38.6 cm x W 31.1 cm x D 2 cm
2000-03595

2

3

4

TIGER BALM GARDEN, SINGAPORE   星加坡萬金油花園

Metal calendars were extremely popular in the 1950s. They could be seen both in the home as well as in coffee shops. Popular local brands such as Axe Brand Oil and Tiger Balm used these calendars as signboards to advertise their goods. The pictures used commonly featured both Caucasian and Asian models who were popular at the time.

1   Kissan Mango Juice calendar, 1950s
     Metal
     H 24.3 cm x W 35.7 cm x D 1 cm
     2000-06913

2   Craven A Calendar, 1950s
     Metal
     H 19 cm x W 27.75 cm x D 1 cm
     1997-02136

3   Tiger Balm calendar, 1950s
     Metal
     H 38 cm x W 25 cm
     2000-07936

4   Calendar, 1957
     Paper
     H 7.8 cm x W 10.8 cm
     2001-03881

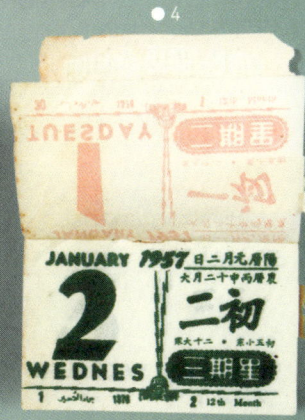

● 1

● 2

● 3

Time out for refreshment

Quality drink the world over—
delicious Coca-Cola

樂 可口可

Coca-Cola

JANUARY 1958 FEBRUARY

1 Calendar, 1955
Paper
H 54.4 cm x W 38.5 cm
2001-03878

2 Calendar holder, 1950s
Paper
H 38.9 cm x W 26.2 cm
Donated by Mak Wai Har
1995-00664

3 Calendar sheet, 1958
Paper
H 21.7 cm x W 15.7 cm
2000-00545

4 Calendar, 1958
Paper
H 56 cm x W 33.1 cm
1994-05686

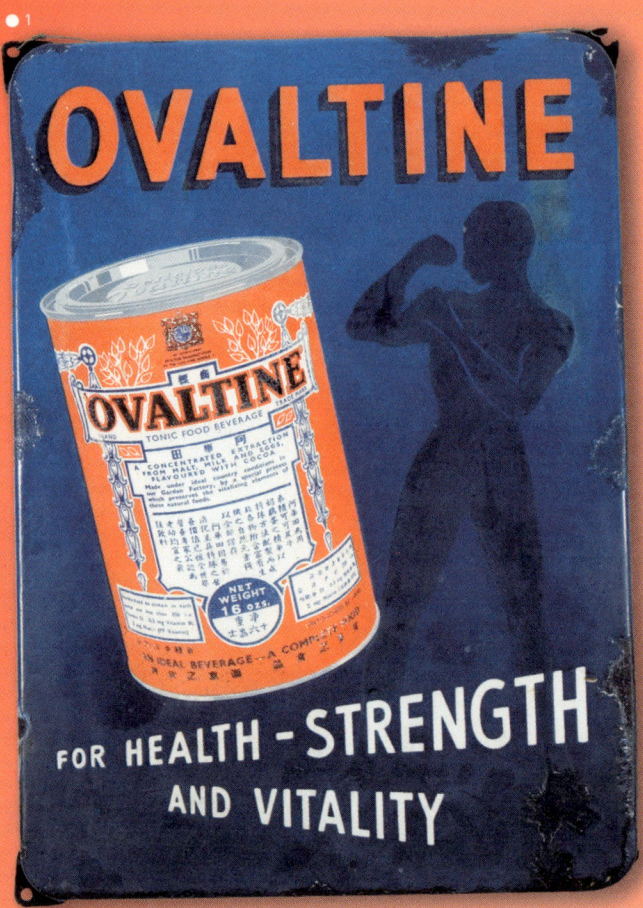

3

4

1 Ovaltine advertisement signboard,
  1950s
  Metal
  H 31 cm x W 43.7 cm
  2000-03554

2 Milkmaid was the single most
  popular brand of condensed milk,
  and was the preferred choice of
  coffee and tea drinkers at coffee
  shops and in the home. Workers
  often took away their drinks in
  empty milkmaid containers.

  Milkmaid advertisement signboard,
  1950s
  Metal
  H 29 cm x W 15 cm
  2000-01555

Beer companies often sponsored metal
signboards and lanterns, which were
displayed at coffee shops.

3 Carlsberg signboard, 1950s
  Metal
  H 49.5 cm x W 33.5 cm
  2000-06586

4 Tiger Beer lantern, 1950s
  Glass, metal and wire
  Lantern,
  H 43.5 cm x W 28 cm x D 28.6 cm
  Wire, L 31.4 cm
  2000-03629

• 1

• 2

Beverage companies commonly used bright colours and bold designs in their advertisements to attract consumers. The trademark red lion on a yellow and red background of the company Fraser and Neave (F & N) became synonymous with soft drinks, which were available in the coffee shops. Founded by John Fraser and David Neave in 1883, F & N was the Singapore and Straits Aerated Water Company before it was renamed in 1889.

• 1   F & N advertisement signboard, 1960s
    Porcelain enamel
    H 48.2 cm x W 64.4 cm
    2000-03557

• 2   F & N drinking glass, 1970s
    Glass
    H 11.7 cm x Diam. 7.4 cm
    1995-05505

• 3   F & N advertisement tray, 1950s
    Enamel
    H 37 cm x Diam. 27 cm
    1995-02297

• 4   F & N drinking glass, 1960s
    Glass
    H 13.1 cm x Diam. 7.8 cm
    1995-05514

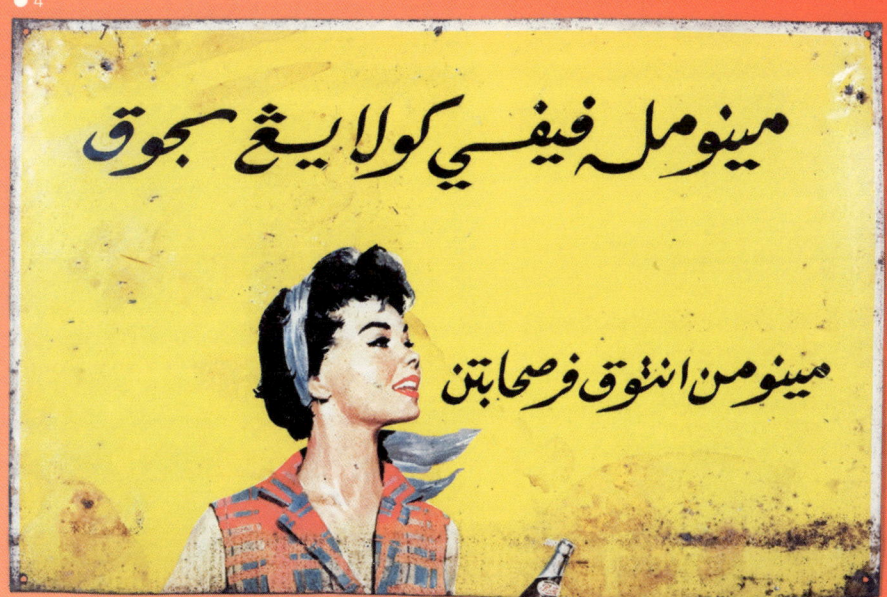

Other soft drinks sold at coffee shops included common brands such as Pepsi Cola, Greenspot, Kickapoo and Framroz. Their packaging was designed to attract the emerging baby boomers and the urban middle class of the 1960s. Brands such as Pepsi Cola produced advertising trays, calendars and thermometers to tap into this "New Generation" (the tagline of Pepsi's most successful advertising campaign) and Asia constituted an important overseas market.

1   Greenspot drinking glasses, 1970s
    Glass
    H 12.4–13.4 cm x Diam. 7.4–7.7 cm
    1995-05500, 1995-05518

2   Greenspot advertising signboard
    with thermometer, 1960s
    Porcelain enamel
    H 40.5 cm x W 12 cm x D 1.3 cm
    1995-05518

3   Amoy Canning advertisement
    signboard, 1960s
    Cardboard
    H 9 cm x W 17.6 cm
    1995-04381

4   Pepsi Cola signboard in
    Urdu, 1950s
    Porcelain enamel
    H 49.6 cm x W 33.5 cm
    2000-08251

5   Pepsi Cola drinking
    glasses, 1960s
    Glass
    H 12.6–3.1 cm x Diam. 7–7.8 cm
    1995-05511, 2000-07803

6   Pepsi Cola advertising signboard
    with thermometer, 1950s
    Porcelain enamel
    H 30.6 cm x W 17 cm
    1995-00476

The soft drink industry took off with the post-World-War-II economic boom. Soft drink consumption increased as Singaporeans became more affluent. Accordingly, the bottling and canning industry rapidly evolved. Glass bottles with metallic caps were used to store the drinks until the aluminum can became widely used in the 1960s. F & N Cola-Cola is Singapore's oldest and largest soft drink manufacturer.

1   Framroz soft drink bottle, 1960s
    Glass
    H 18.4 cm x Diam. 5.5 cm
    1995-10598

2   Eastern Cola soft drink
    bottle, 1960s
    Glass
    H 20 cm x Diam. 5 cm
    1995-10666

3   Long Bros. A. W. soft drink
    bottle, 1960s
    Glass
    H 23.7 cm x Diam. 6.1 cm
    2001-06690

4   Suka soft drink bottle, 1960s
    Glass
    H 23 cm x Diam. 5.7 cm
    1995-10674

5   Eastern Aerated Water soft drink
    bottle, 1960s
    Glass
    H 23.5 cm x D 6.1 cm
    2001-06685

6   Fraser & Neave soft drink
    bottle, 1960s
    Glass
    H 24 cm x Diam. 6.5 cm
    2001-06693

● 1

● 2

● 3

State Express 555 was one of the most popular brands of cigarettes in Singapore in the post-World-War-II period.

1   State Express 555 cigarette advertisement signboard, 1950s
Enamel
H 60.5 cm x W 45 cm
2000-03551

2   State Express 555 cigarette can, 1950s
Tin
H 10.8 cm x Diam. 6.9 cm
1995-08029

3   State Express 555 cigarette box, 1940s
Tin
H 8.9 cm x W 7.7 cm x D 1.8 cm
1995-08185

4   Marlboro cigarette can, 1950s
Tin
H 8.9 cm x Diam. 6.9 cm
1995-08076

5   Piccadilly Number One cigarette can, 1950s
Tin
H 7.7 cm x Diam. 7.3 cm
1995-08030

6   Piccadilly Number One cigarette box, 1940s
Tin
H 11.3 cm x W 7.7 cm x D 1.7 cm
1995-08167

Most brands of cigarettes, which were sold in coffee shops and sundry shops across Singapore in the 1950s, were imported from the United Kingdom. Many of the brands seen here reflect the smoking preferences of the British smokers who lived and worked in Singapore.

○ 1   Golden Dragons cigarette
       can, 1950s
       Tin
       H 8.4 cm x Diam. 7 cm
       1995-08021

○ 2   St. Moritz cigarette can, 1950s
       Tin
       H 8.7 cm x Diam. 6.9 cm
       1995-08028

○ 3   Churchman's cigarette can, 1950s
       Tin
       H 8 cm x Diam. 7.5 cm
       1995-08033

○ 4   Ardath cigarette can, 1950s
       Tin
       H 7.2 cm x Diam. 6.8 cm
       1995-08022

○ 5   Gold Flake Cigarettes advertisment
       signboard, 1950s
       Enamel
       H 56 cm x W 43.2 cm
       2000-03553

89

SINGAPORE
CHILDHOOD

SINGAPORE CHILDHOOD

The collection highlights the simple pleasures of a childhood in Singapore; it shows a time that was typically carefree, when children were mostly left to their own devices.

he museum's collection of artefacts relating to
hildhood is very new in comparison to the other
ollections. Indeed the development of family
istory is relatively short in Singapore. The notion
 the 'perfect' family in Singapore at the turn of the
ventieth century can be seen through the studio
ortraits of wealthy Europeans, Eurasians, Indians,
alays, Chinese and Peranakans who were living
 material comfort with their children and
embers of their extended family.

   The population of Singapore during the
neteenth century was mainly composed of
migrant male workers from India and China.
ese men had neither the means nor the intention
 start families and few saw Singapore as their
me. To many, Singapore was nothing more than
ransient place in which to work and to make
oney. The instability of world politics and the
rld economy in the 1930s meant that these
migrant men were not able to travel in and out

Providing a safe place for
children to play, the Singapore
Red Cross Centre was
established in 1949.

of Singapore easily. However, things soon changed and by the 1950s, the population of women in Singapore had increased due to a surge in female immigration. As a result, the working classes began to marry, family formation became more prevalent and, in turn, Singapore's population began to stabilise. Thus, artefacts relating to familial life and children only became more readily available from this period onwards.

The museum's collection on childhood falls into three main categories. The first is concerned with the school-going culture. The second is related to play, and the last features the efforts of the Post Office Savings Bank (POSB) to foster good saving habits in children.

Relating to the first category, the museum purchased a collection of school badges and, in 1995, received a donation of school textbooks that were used in schools in the 1950s and 1960s. These artefacts reflect a shift in educational policy as well as a distinct change in the school-going culture. In the post-World-War-II period, educational policy

A vivid, and shared, memory of childhood is the annual class photograph; this example is from Raffles Girls' School, taken during the 1960s.

was for schools to provide English-medium education for all, and to encourage parents to send their children to those schools that charged lower fees. Parents were implicitly discouraged from sending their children to the Chinese-medium schools, over which the government had little control. In 1959, 47 per cent of children entering primary schools were registered in English-medium schools. Twenty years later in 1979, the rate had risen to 91 per cent.

This drastic shift was partly due to the increased number of job opportunities for those who were fluent in English. While English was given priority as the language of international business, the government's policy also acknowledged the importance of the mother tongue. To develop and maintain a strong cultural identity of the new generation of locally born Singaporeans, bilingual education was made compulsory at the primary level in 1960 and at secondary level in 1966.

In 1947, statistics show that 60 per cent of the population was locally born, and by the 1950s,

the 'baby boom' was in full swing. During 1966, a total of 39,835 babies were delivered at Kandang Kerbau Hospital, a record-breaking figure. The hospital duly made it to the Guinness Book of Records for delivering the most babies in a maternity facility that year.

Making up the second category of the childhood artefacts, the museum's collection includes simple toys such as the wooden rocking horse, 'Pick-Up-Sticks', and toy cars. Gathered through acquisition and donations made in the late 1990s and early 2000s, these toys reflect a bygone era of simple pleasures. This part of the collection also consists of various comics and picture books that were published between the 1940s and 1960s. These popular books captured the attention of the young with characters such as Enid Blyton's *Mary Mouse*.

During the 1960s and 1970s, the Post Office Savings Bank introduced the 'Squirrel Savers' Club. It was almost a rite of passage for children aged six and above, especially in the 1970s, to be brought by their parents to the bank to open their first savings account. Upon opening one, money boxes were given to encourage children to save their pocket money. Once the money boxes were full, the money was deposited in their very own bank account.

This page: Children during Education Week in 1950.

Opposite: The simple pleasures of childhood highlighted by the communal spirit of the *kampong*.

This page from top: A baby
photographed in the Botanic
Gardens in 1939; an ice cream
cart; the sack race during the
Social Welfare Childrens' Sports
Day in 1953.

Opposite from top: A family day-
trip to the Chinese Garden;
children enjoying the outdoors;
Western fashion was favoured
for children as well as adults.

1

1 School badges, 1950s to 1970s
Metal
H 2.6–5 cm x 2.3–4.1 cm
First column from top; 1995-06212,
1995-06290, 1995-06434, 1995-
06426, 1995-07651, 1995-06225.
Second column from top; 1995-
06423, 1995-06230, 1995-07892,
1995-06817, 1995-06412.
Third column from top; 1995-06167,
1995-07715, 1995-06273, 1995-06301,
1995-07093, 1995-06407.
Fourth column from top; 1995-
07097, 1995-07617, 1995-06235,
1995-06177, 1995-07363

2 SPS Head Prefect
badge, 1950s
Metal
H 3.4 cm x W 3.2 cm
1995-06442

3 St. Andrew's School Monitor
badge, 1950s
Metal
H 3.8 cm x W 4.1 cm
1995-07613

4 School Bands Major Proficiency
badge, 1950s
Metal
H 5 cm x D 0.4 cm
1995-06208

5 Tanglin Girls' School badge, 1950s
Metal
H 2.8 cm x W 2.5 cm
1995-06289

● 1

● 4

● 1 *General Mathematics for Malayan Schools Vol I to IV*, school textbooks, 1950s to 1960s
Paper
H 18.7 cm x W 13 cm x D 2.3 cm
Donated by Wendy Hitchell-Jones née Wendy Toh Kim Kee
2006-00350-3

● 2 *Mengapa Belajar Bahasa Kebangsaan* (Why Learn the National Language), school textbook, 1950s to 1960s
Paper
H 20.3 cm x W 15.3 cm
1995-00373

● 3 *Belajar Bahasa Kita* (Learn Our Language), school textbook, 1950s to 1960s
Paper
H 20.4 cm x W 15 cm
1995-00367

● 4 *English Progress Books for Malayans*, school textbook, 1950s to 1960s
Paper
H 27.8 cm x W 20.6 cm
Donated by Tan Hien Wah
1995-00108

● 5 *Junior Malayan Geographies*, school textbook, 1950s to 1960s
Paper
H 22.7 cm x W 15.4 cm
Donated by Tan Hien Wah
1995-00093

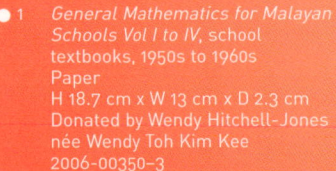

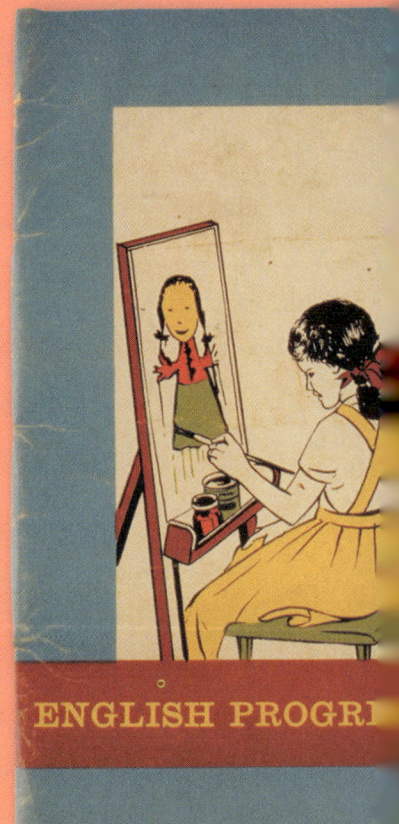

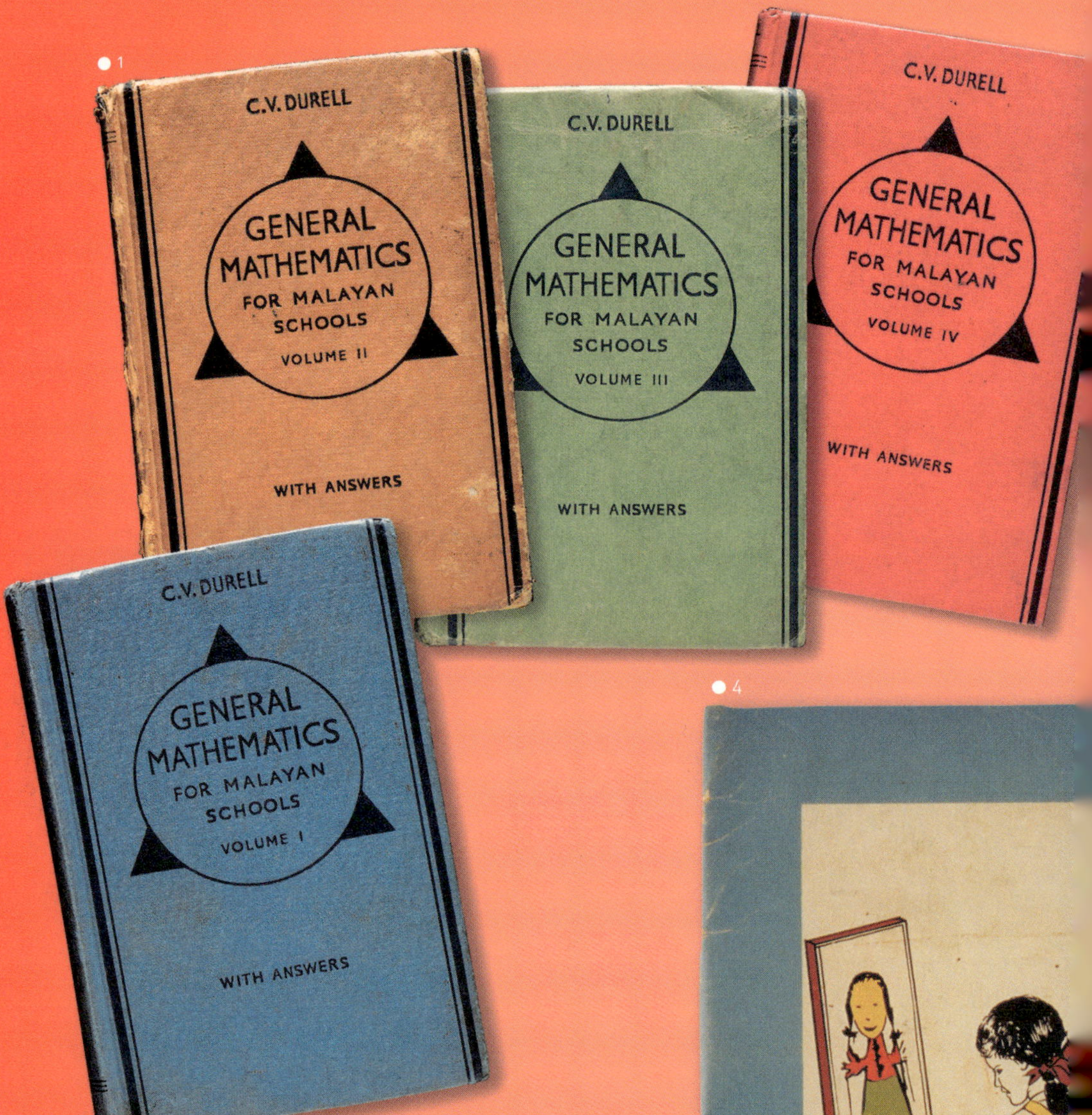

2

Rampaizan Kĕbudayan Malaya (Jilid II)
馬來亞文化叢書（第二集）

Mĕngapa Bĕlajar
Bahasa Kĕbangsaan

为甚麼学習國語

星洲維明公司出版

3

BBK

BĔLAJAR
BAHASA
KITA

BUKU III

Oleh
HARUN AMINURRASHID

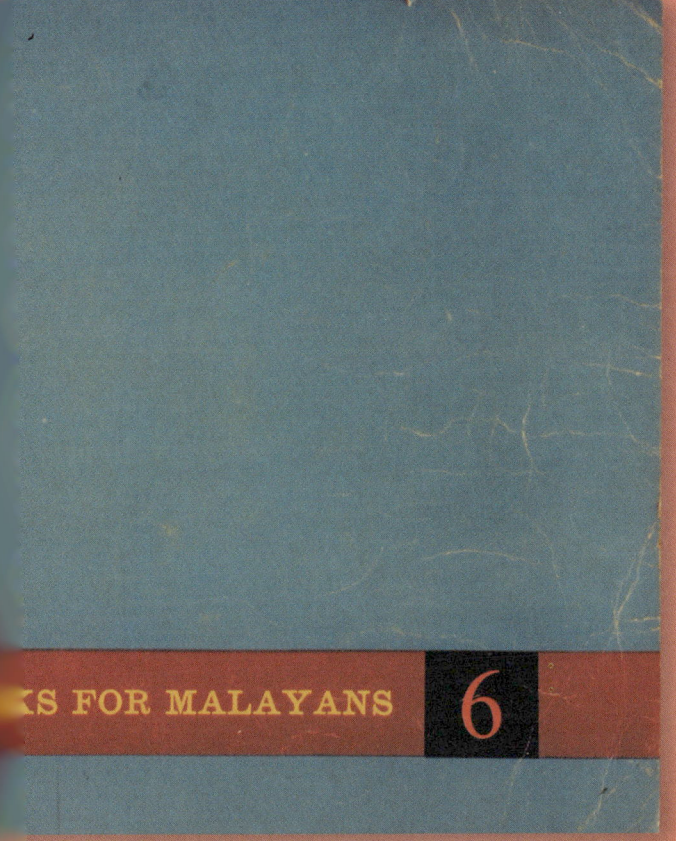

KS FOR MALAYANS 6

5

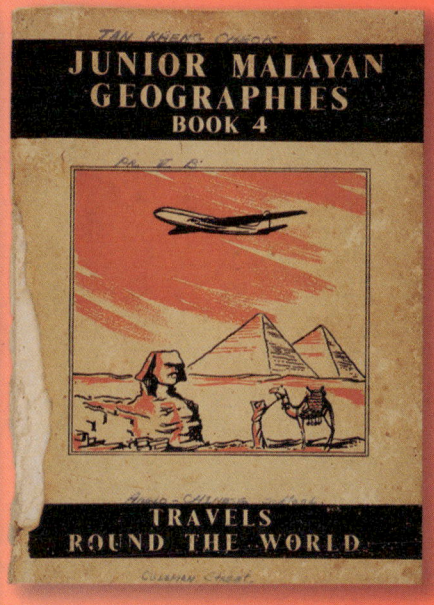

JUNIOR MALAYAN
GEOGRAPHIES
BOOK 4

TRAVELS
ROUND THE WORLD

1

THE LITTLE BLACK CHICK

Reader 3
Structural English Course

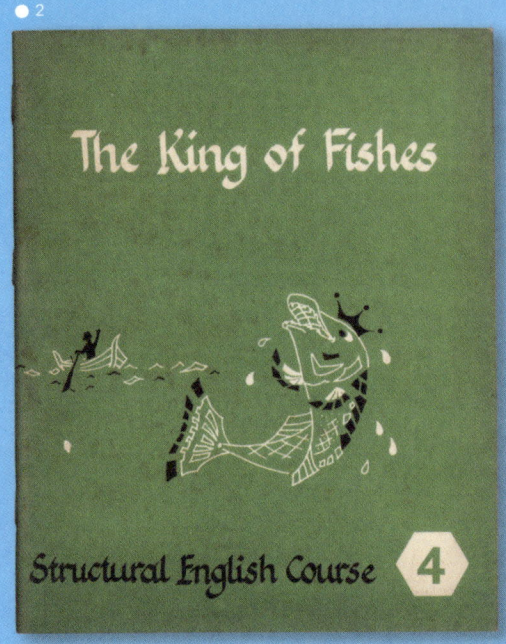

2

The King of Fishes

Structural English Course 4

3

At the Zoo

Structural English Course 5

4

Ali and his Kite

Structural English Course 6

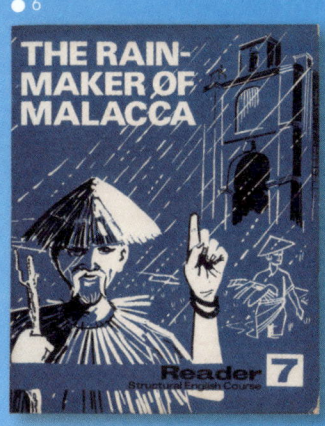

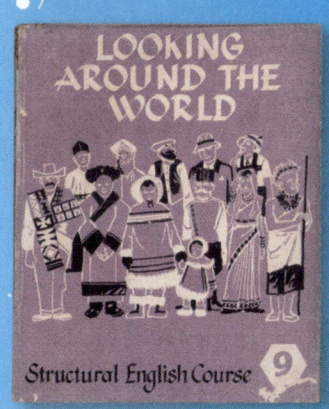

1 *The Little Black Chick,*
   Structural English Course,
   school textbook, 1960s
   Paper
   H 21 cm x W 16.9 cm
   Reserve collection

2 *The King of Fishes,*
   Structural English Course,
   school textbook, 1960s
   Paper
   H 21 cm x W 16.9 cm
   Reserve collection

3 *At the Zoo, Structural English*
   Course, school textbook, 1960s
   Paper

   H 21 cm x W 16.9 cm
   Reserve collection

4 *Ali and his Kite, Structural English*
   Course, school textbook, 1960s
   Paper
   H 21 cm x W 16.9 cm
   Reserve collection

5 *Adventure on Kusu Island,*
   Structural English Course,
   school textbook, 1960s
   Paper
   H 21 cm x W 16.9 cm
   Donated by Tan Hien Wah
   1995-00123

6 *The Rainmaker of Malacca,*
   Structural English Course,
   school textbook, 1960s
   Paper
   H 21 cm x W 16.9 cm
   Donated by Tan Hien Wah
   1995-00105

7 *Looking Around the World,*
   Structural English Course,
   school textbook, 1960s
   Paper
   H 21 cm x W 16.9 cm
   Reserve collection

1 Toy ballerina, 1950s
   Plastic
   H 6 cm x W 4.3 cm x D 2 cm
   Donated by Quek Yuen Yuan, Ana
   1997-00582

2 Pick-up sticks, 1950s
   Plastic
   Container, H 20.8 cm x Diam. 4.8 cm
   Sticks, H 15.5 cm x Diam. 0.3 cm
   Donated by Quek Yuen Yuan, Ana
   1997-00577

3 Rocking horse, 1950s
   Painted metal
   H 42.8 cm x W 36.2 cm x D 68.2 cm
   1995-01682

4 Rocking horse, 1950s
   Wood
   H 36.4 cm x W 27.8 cm x D 68.6 cm
   1995-01681

3

4

The Matchbox series of toys was a faithful companion for many boys during their childhood, some of whom probably became die-cast toy collectors in adulthood. The line of toys was introduced in 1953 and, since 1960, 75 models of such miniature toys have been made each year. Competition from other toy manufacturers in the 1970s ensured Matchbox's innovation, which led them to introduce low friction cars that ran faster.

● 1   Lesney Matchbox No. 73 Ferrari F1
       Racing Car, 1962
       Die-cast
       H 2.8 cm x W 3.9 cm x D 7.1 cm
       1998-00005

● 2   Lesney Matchbox Superfast No. 21
       Renault 5TL, 1978
       Die-cast
       H 2.6 cm x W 3.9 cm x D 8.1 cm
       1998-00006

● 3   Lesney Matchbox No. 53 Flareside
       Pickup, 1982
       Die-cast
       H 3.7 cm x W 3.9 cm x D 8.1 cm
       1998-00008

● 4   Lesney Matchbox No. 3 Bedford
       Tipper Truck, 1961
       Die-cast
       H 2.7 cm x W 3.9 cm x D 6.8 cm
       1998-00009

● 5   Lesney Matchbox Superfast No. 27
       Lamborghini Countach, 1973
       Die-cast
       H 2.6 cm x W 3.9 cm x D 7.8 cm
       1998-00007

● 6   Lesney Matchbox No. 51 Pontiac
       Firebird, 1982
       Die-cast
       H 3.6 cm x W 3.9 cm x D 8 cm
       1998-00010

● 7   Lesney Matchbox No. 75 Seasprite
       Helicopter, 1978
       Die-cast
       H 2.7 cm x W 3.9 cm x D 8.2 cm
       1998-00011

1 Knife, 1960s
Plastic
H 53.5 cm x W 6.8 cm
Donated by Quek Yuen Yuan, Ana
1997-00634

2 Slingshot, 1950s
Mixed material
H 21.5 cm x W 12.5 cm x D 27 cm
Donated by Wong Yoke Ching
1999-00210

3 Pop gun, 1950s
Mixed material
H 7.5 cm x W 21.5 cm
1995-04422-001

4 Sword, 1960s
Plastic
H 72 cm x W 9 cm
Donated by Quek Yuen Yuan, Ana
1997-00633

左輪槍
POP GUN

3

4

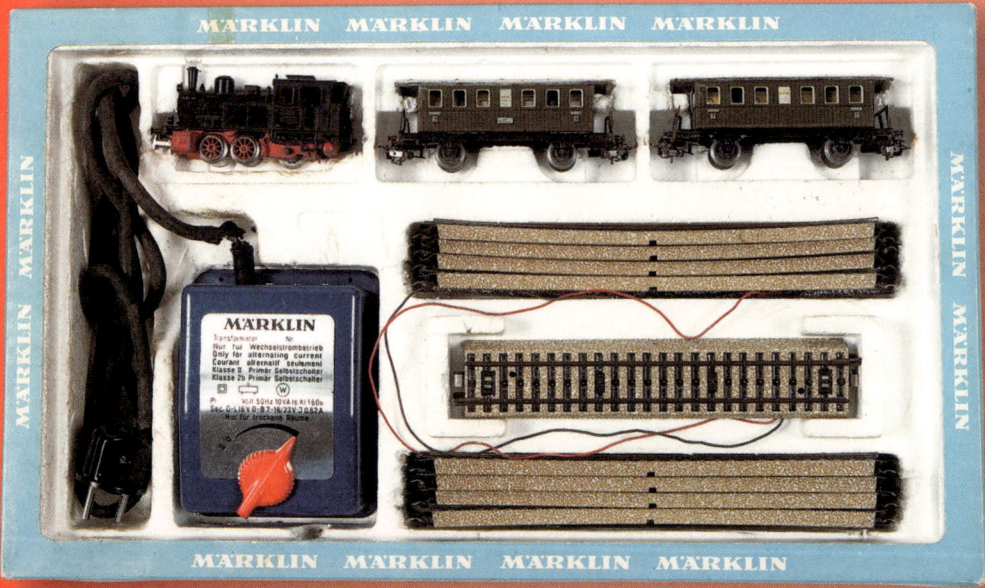

1   Marklin passenger train set,
        Circa 1965
        Metal
        H 47 cm x W 28 cm x D 7.3 cm
        Donated by Low Wye Mun
        1997-00574

2   Doctor set, 1960s
        Plastic
        H 27 cm x W 19.4 cm
        1995-04425

DOctor set

ABSORBENT COTTON

Playing Medicine

children hospital

'ASPRO'

for headache, pain, colds & 'flu

Smart toys

For Children Over 3 Years Old

MADE IN HONGKONG

1

2

Tikam games were a popular pastime for young children in the 1950s. Usually these games could be played for 5 cents and prizes were often sweets.

1   *Tikam* (Game of Luck), 1950s
Paper
H 72.3 cm x W 39.1 cm
2002-00975

2   *Tikam* (Game of Luck), 1950s
Paper
H 55.8 cm x W 38.9 cm
2002-00977

3   *Tikam* (Game of Luck), 1950s
Paper
H 56.2 cm x W 38.9 cm
2002-00972

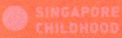

1

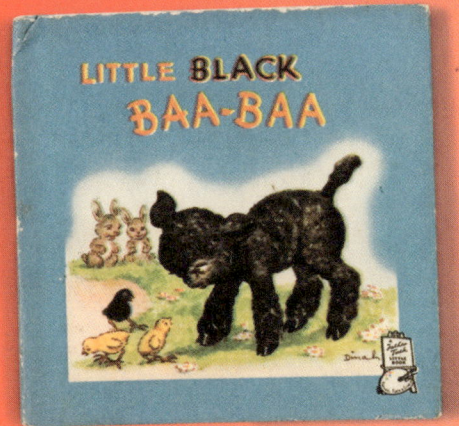

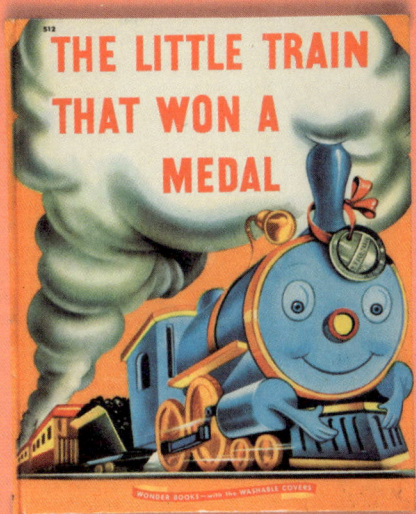

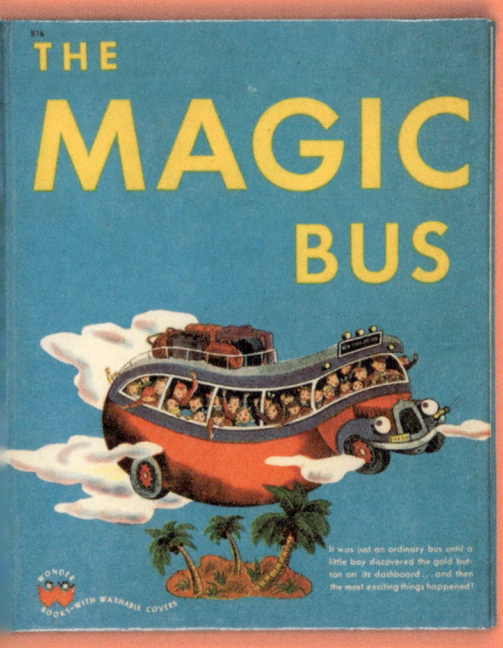

ese storybooks and comics managed to
pture children's imaginations during the
st-World-War-II years. Popular authors
ch as Jane Pilgrim and Enid Blyton
eated delightful characters, including
grim's *Blackberry Farm* animals and
yton's *Mary Mouse* resulting in timeless
es that enthralled generations of
ldren. Paper shortages during and after
e war meant such publications were

cheaply made with simple colour
illustrations and stapled bindings.

● 1　Assorted storybooks by various
English authors, 1940s to 1950s
Paper
H 10.7–18.8 cm x W 10.7–12.9 cm
Donated by Quek Kai Miew
2004-00372, 2004-00413, 2004-00371,
2004-00396, 2004-00388, 2004-00369

● 2　Assorted storybooks by various
English authors, 1940s to 1950s
Paper
H 20.8 cm x W 16.7 cm
Donated by Quek Kai Miew
2004-00401, 2004-00408,
2004-00405, 2004-00403

● 1

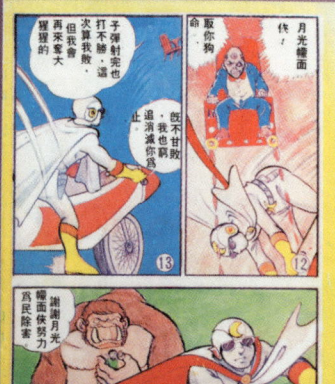

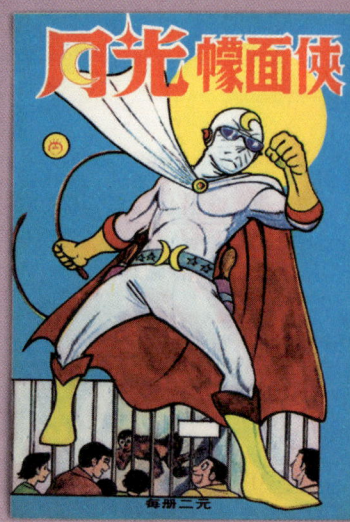

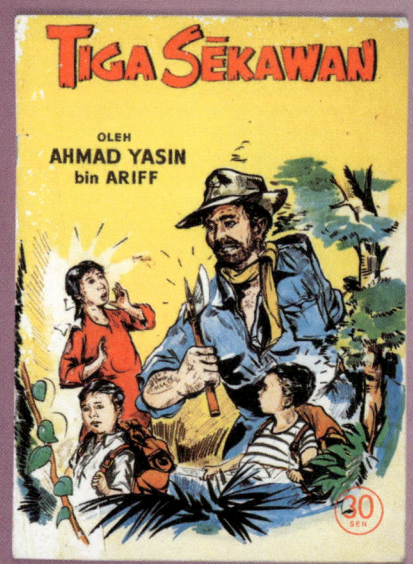

● 1 Assorted Malay and Chinese comic
books, 1940s to 1950s
Paper
H 18.9–26.5 cm x W 12.7–18.9 cm
1997-00671, 1997-00672, 2001-05209,
2001-05208

● 2 Assorted storybooks by English and
Chinese authors, 1940s to 1950s
Paper
H 7.1–23.6 cm x W 15.2–17 cm
Donated by Quek Kai Miew
2004-00428, 2004-00422,
2004-00415, 2004-00385,
2004-00383, 2004-00386

Assorted storybooks by various authors,
...0s to 1950s
...per
...–20.8 cm x W 15.3–16.6 cm
...ated by Quek Kai Miew
...04-00369, 2004-00371, 2004-00374,
...04-00375, 2004-00377, 2004-00379,
...04-00380, 2004-00384, 2004-00391,
...04-00394, 2004-00404, 2004-00409,
...04-00410, 2004-00412, 2004-00414, 2004-
...18, 2004-00421, 2004-00424, 2004-00426

1

POSBank 25th Anniversary Commemorative Souvenirs

FRONT DESIGN
*POSBank staff at work at the Bank's
model branch at Suntec City.*

ILLUSTRATOR
Loy Chye Chuan

MEDIUM
Water-colour

VALUE OF CARD
S$2.00

SIZE OF CARD
54mm x 86mm

FRONT DESIGN
*Smiley Squirrel, POSBank's mascot
for the Schools' Savings Campaign.*

ILLUSTRATOR
Jumali Katani

MEDIUM
Water-colour

VALUE OF CARD
S$2.00

SIZE OF CARD
54mm x 86mm

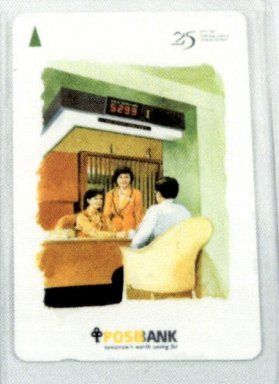

Urging saving practices in young children, these money boxes and savings club ephemera—and other artefacts donated by POSBank in 2001—reflect an important phase of a Singaporean childhood and the coming-of-age of Singapore itself.

1 POSBash folder, 1997
   Paper
   H 20.1 cm x W 11.6 cm
   Donated by POSB Centre
   2001-01071

2 Bugs Bunny, with POSB logo,
   sticker, 1970s
   Paper
   Diam. 8.9 cm
   Donated by POSB Centre
   2001-00793

3 I Love You Daddy fridge
   magnet, 1970s
   Plastic
   H 12 cm x W 9.3 cm x D 0.2 cm
   Donated by POSB Centre
   2001-00850

4 Gold squirrel badge, 1970s
   Metal
   H 3.2 cm x W 3.9 cm
   Donated by POSB Centre
   2001-01037

5 Green squirrel badge, 1970s
   Metal
   Diam. 4.3 cm
   Donated by POSB Centre
   2001-01037

6 Orange squirrel badge, 1970s
   Metal
   Diam. 5.5 cm
   Donated by POSB Centre
   2001-00919

7 Squirrel T-shirt, 1970s
   Cotton
   H 86.1 cm x W 70.5 cm
   Donated by POSB Centre
   2001-00877

4

5

6

1   Mushroom with squirrel face money
box, 1970s
Ceramic
H 12 cm x W 9.2 cm x D 3.5 cm
Donated by POSB Centre
2001-00386

2   Squirrel sitting on books money
box, 1970s
Ceramic
H 17 cm x W 14.2 cm x D 8 cm
Donated by POSB Centre
2001-00421

3   Squirrel money box, 1970s
Ceramic
H 17 cm x W 9.5 cm x D 12 cm
Donated by POSB Centre
2001-00409

4   House money box, 1970s
Ceramic
H 16 cm x W 10.5 cm x D 12.3 cm
Donated by POSB Centre
2001-00411

5   Nutbase money box, 1970s
Ceramic
H 13.7 cm x W 9.2 cm x D 9.7 cm
Donated by POSB Centre
2001-00384

6   Rectangular Squirrel Savers' Club
money box, 1970s
Ceramic
H 14 cm x W 9.2 cm x D 10.8 cm
Donated by POSB Centre
2001-00398

● 1 Apple money box, 1970s
Ceramic
H 6.2 cm x W 6.3 cm x D 6.5 cm
Donated by POSB Centre
2001-00401

● 2 Gold money box, 1980s
Metal
H 10 cm x W 17.5 cm x D 6 cm
Donated by POSB Centre
2001-00382

● 3 Cash-on-line machine
money box, 1980s
Ceramic
H 13.9 cm x W 9.5 cm x D 10.6 cm
Donated by POSB Centre
2001-00414

● 4 Centenary passbook design money
box, 1980s
Ceramic
H 13.7 cm x W8.8 cm x D 12.5 cm
2001-00393

● 5 Merlion money box, 1980s
Ceramic
H 25 cm x W 8.1 cm x D 13 cm
Donated by POSB Centre
2001-00413

5

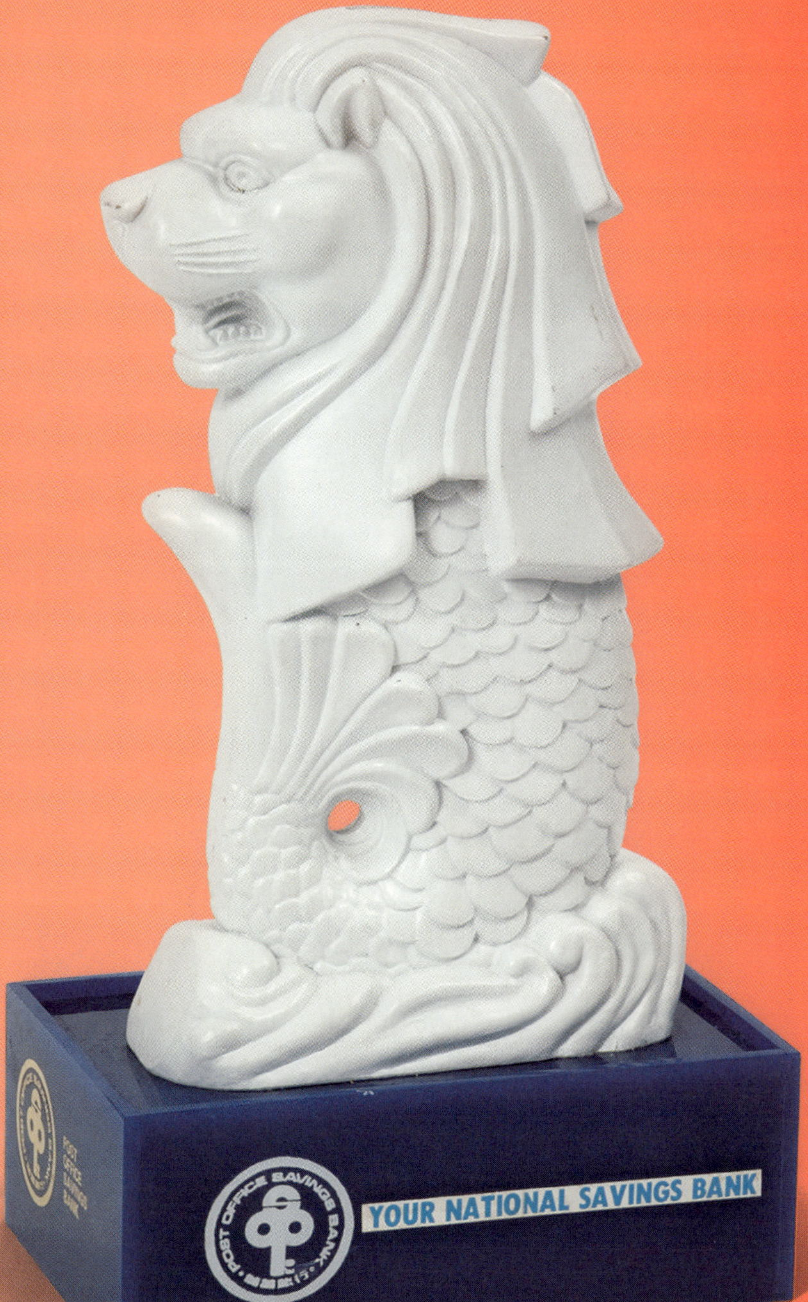
POST OFFICE SAVINGS BANK
YOUR NATIONAL SAVINGS BANK

SINGAPORE
STYLE

SINGAPORE STYLE

The post-war years were a period of immense change, and nowhere was this more apparent than in the fashion world, where new styles were regularly introduced by Singapore's modern women.

The role and identity of Singaporean women underwent marked changes in the period from the 1950s to the 1970s. As the economy boomed during the 1960s, more and more women left their homemaker roles to join the labour force. For the first time, women gained an earning power. In turn, as their spending increased, they became an important group of consumers for the fashion and beauty industry. These drastic social changes saw the collapse of the old world order, and induced distinct changes in the Singaporean lifestyle. The youth movement, largely influenced by Western popular culture, emerged from the 1950s 'baby boom' era with new tastes in fashion that would challenge conventions.

Perhaps most significantly, the Westernised form-fitting style of dress started to replace the traditional loose-fitting Asian silhouette in the 1950s. By the 1960s, fashion preferences had become increasingly globalised. Women in

Guests at Thailand's centenary celebrations held in 1964, at the Cathay Restaurant, are entertained by a modern fashion show.

Singapore were not only consumers of fashion; many worked in the garment industry during this period. Until mass-produced garments and synthetic fabrics became the norm in the 1970s, women preferred tailor-made clothes and even made their own. Many women used their dressmaking skills to update traditional Asian garments with modern, Western styles and fabrics, creating a distinctive hybridised look. Constantly seeking inspiration from broader cultural trends, women could refer to local magazines, as well as Hollywood and Hong Kong films, for tips on wardrobe coordination and beauty.

Even though women's social status was beginning to change, they were still expected to dress appropriately by covering certain parts of their body during particular occasions. Some fashion innovations, such as the miniskirt, raised concerns about women's modesty. Nevertheless, resourceful women found ways, and had the skills, to adapt these global fashion trends while at the same time appeasing the traditionalists.

Keen to perfect their look, women would often queue to get the latest fashionable hairstyles, such as the beehive.

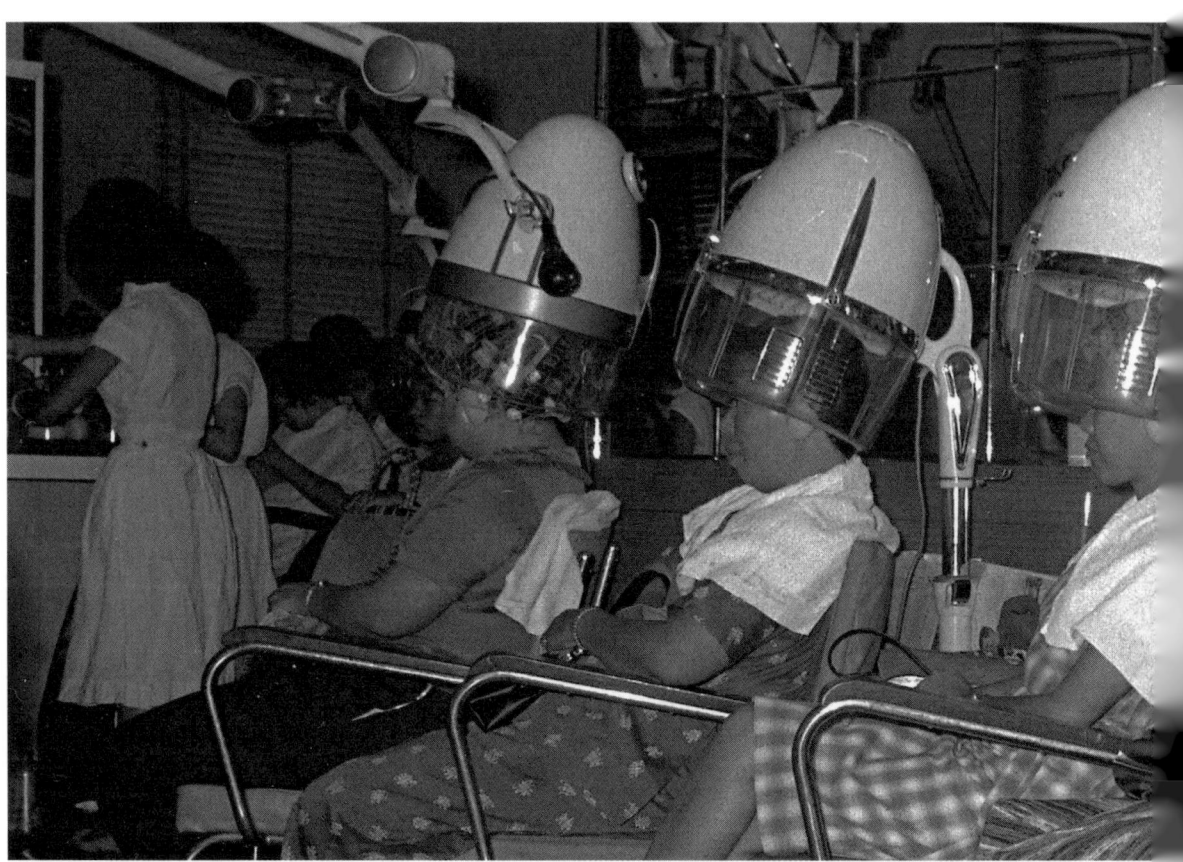

The museum's extensive collection includes a variety of garments and accessories such as bags, jewellery and shoes, as well as cosmetic products. These artefacts, not only illustrate the sense of style during this period, they also show that women had the resources to achieve the desirable look.

The collection of bags ranges from large practical handbags to delicate evening clutches. For work and shopping, large plain handbags made of leather and suede were preferred. For excursions, lunchbox-style bags were popular. For evening, women opted for feminine-looking clutches made of luxurious fabrics such as satin, which were usually decorated with diamanté or crystals.

Another important fashion accessory are shoes. A large part of the collection, comprising high-quality custom-made leather and suede shoes, was donated by Madam Wu Chuen Chuen, who ran Stamford Café, located along Bras Basah Road from the 1950s to the 1970s. In addition, there are some platform shoes that were very much in vogue during the early 1970s.

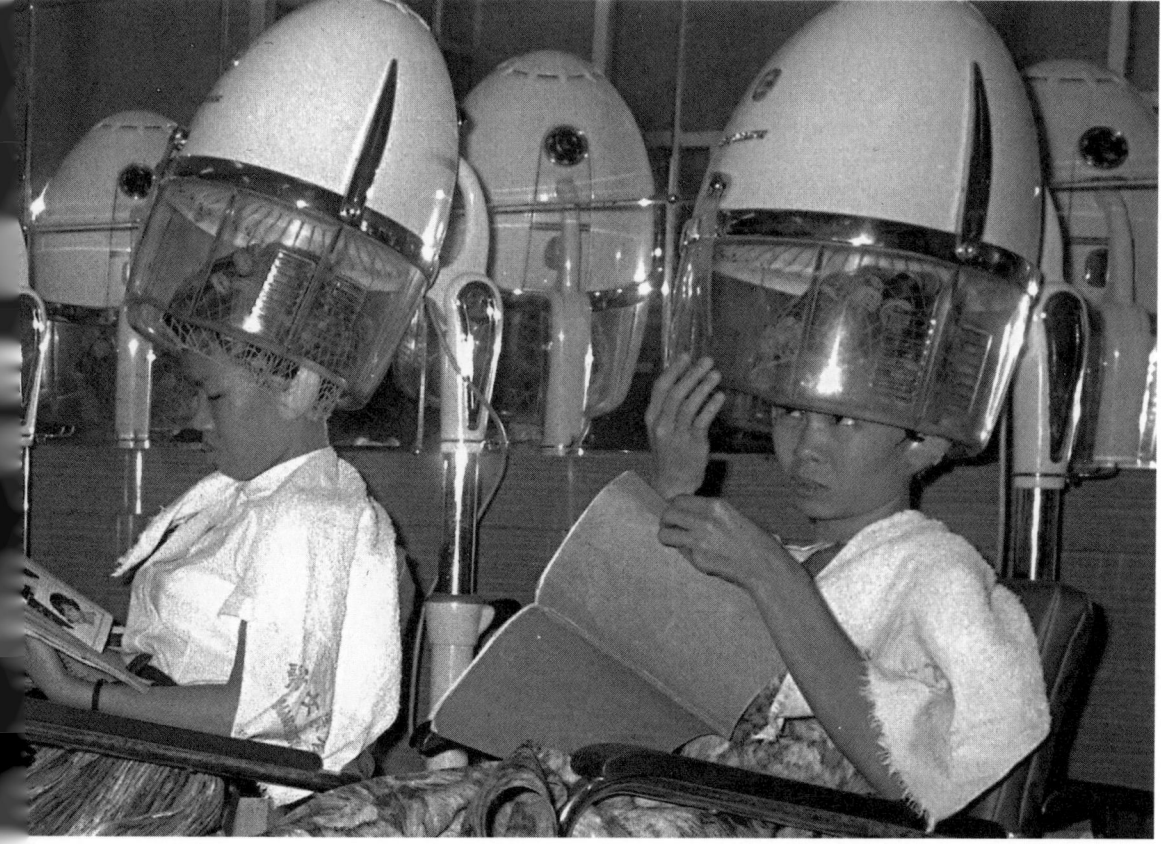

Women's fashions are shown at
the YWCA Fashion Show held at
the Conference Hall in 1966.

Bright and bold plastic jewellery, such as the earrings and flower brooches on pages 158–159, were the hallmarks of fashion. Wigs and hairpieces, which could be twisted into knots, gathered in a ponytail or puffed out in a bouffant, were also important in completing the look. Hair curlers, combs, hairgrips and hairsprays were commonly used to style and tease hairpieces into shape. In addition, hairdryers (see page 184) became important electrical appliances in the 1950s and 1960s for women sporting the beehive.

Spectacles completed the look. Black and brown cat's-eye frames were a must-have in the 1950s. This trend soon changed and by the late 1960s, oversized sunglasses of various colours and shapes became the dominant trend.

The collection would be incomplete without the cosmetic products of the era. They include locally produced varieties of face powder and eau de toilette such as 'Butterfly' and 'Girl' Florida water. These brands were very popular, as were imported products, such as 'Max Factor' perfumes and powders, 'Revlon' lipsticks and 'Coty' perfumes. Departmental stores such as Robinsons, John Little and Whiteaways were the main emporiums from which newly prosperous women would purchase these imported beauty products.

This page from top: Day-trips to the park were the ideal occasion to dress up; fashionable swimwear on display at Singapore Swimming Club in 1964; the latest styles at a fashion show in 1966.

Opposite from top: A beauty contest at Gay World in 1969; different styles come together at a Dinner and Dance in 1958; beauty care the old-fashioned way: here the old style of hair removal is demonstrated.

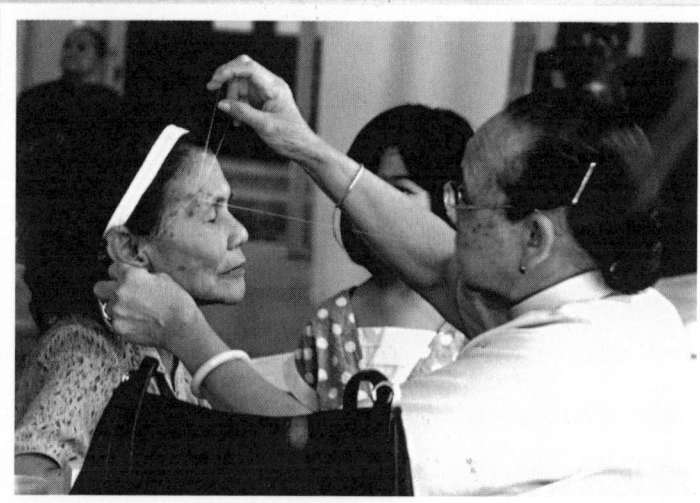

1   Semi circular bag, Late 1960s
     Straw and metal
     H 25.5 cm x W 25.3 cm x D 15 cm
     Donated by Lim Chio May
     2005-00199

2   Brown box-style handbag, 1950s
     Cane and metal
     H 14.9 cm x W 20.1 cm x D 9 cm
     Donated by Low Suet Hing
     2005-00350

3   This acrylic handbag, with diamanté design along the clasp, made an ideal evening bag. It could be worn with any type of garment from Western-style clothing to the more traditional *cheongsam*, *sarong kebaya* or the *sari*. Plastic was used to make handbags of all shapes and sizes, especially during the 1950s and 1960s. This handbag is in an unusually good condition, as plastic tends to crack, chip and warp easily.

     Handbag, Late 1960s
     Acrylic, diamanté and metal
     H 32.4 cm x W 23 cm x D 11 cm
     Donated by Nancy Lim
     2005-01197

4   Red lunchbox bag, 1950s to 1960s
     Plastic and leather
     H 12.8 cm x W 23.4 cm x D 12.6 cm
     Donated by Low Suet Hing
     2005-00349

5

6

7

During the 1950s and 1960s, the clutch or *pochette* was one of several types of bags carried by Singaporean women. Either tucked under the arm or handheld, the clutch was typically used as an evening bag due to its slim shape with space for very few contents such as money or a handkerchief. These clutch bags are made entirely of beads to create different floral patterns. Introduced in 1916, the clutch was revived in the 1950s as a divergence from the more common shoulder bag.

5 Purple and gold beaded
clutch, 1950s
Beads, metal and nylon lining
H 10 cm x W 20 cm
Donated by Oh Beng Swee
2004-00056

6 Red and white beaded clutch
with floral motifs, 1950s
Wooden beads and metal
H 8 cm x W 22 cm x D 4.5 cm
Donated by Rosaini bte Haris
1995-05248

7 Beaded clutch with floral
motifs, 1950s
Wooden beads, nylon lining
and metal
H 18.3 cm x W 35 cm x D 7.5 cm
Donated by Low Suet Hing
2005-00383

1

2

3

1 After World War II, a leather shortage meant different fabrics such as velvet, cotton and rayon were used to make bags. Stepping out of traditional homemaker roles during the 1950s and 1960s, Singaporean women required big and practical bags. The tote bag, which is adapted from the basic paper shopping bag, was the ideal choice for work and shopping.

Red tote with metal clasp, 1970
Raffia, metal, plastic and
nylon lining
H 22.6 cm x W 35 cm x D 12 cm
Donated by Rani Arumugan
2005-01274

2 A delicate wristlet bag, enlivened with diamanté on satin, was the ideal accessory for ladies attending an evening function. Wristlets are characterised by a handle attached to the top centre of the bag. This keeps its weight balanced as the bag dangles gracefully from the wearer's wrist.

Evening bag, 1960s
Satin, diamanté and metal
H 29.3 cm x W 20 cm x D 4 cm
Donated by Irene Hoe
2004-00479

3 Black and white beaded bag, 1960s
Velvet, beads, wood, metal, plastic
and synthetic lining
H 7 cm x W 40.5 cm x D 36.5 cm
Donated by Irene Hoe
2004-00651

4 Black beaded tote, 1960s
Beads, cotton and metal
H 35 cm x W 43 cm x D 2.7 cm
Donated by Irene Hoe
2004-00650

5 Bob bag with a mini purse, 1960s
Velvet and metal
H 41 cm x W 21.3 cm x D 5.2 cm
Donated By Irene Hoe
2004-00480

4

5

1

1. This colourful, medium-sized suitcase is made of durable fabric and comes complete with side padlock and interior straps. Decorated with mod-style floral motifs, it reflects the typical 1960s taste. As there were more opportunities for women to travel abroad for work and leisure, these kinds of cases were a hit among fashionable Singaporean women.

Suitcase, Japan, 1960s
Jute, nylon, polyester and metal
H 37.5 cm x W 54.5 cm x D 13 cm
2006-00801

2. Gucci handbag, 1970s
Leather and metal
H 52.5 cm x W 35 cm x D 8 cm
Donated by Irene Hoe
2004-00654

3. Black handbag, 1960s
Leather and metal
H 30 cm x W 26 cm
Donated by Rosaini bte Haris
1995-05247

4. This black handbag, featuring a long gold strap, stitch detail and tassel, is typical of the 1970s disco fashion. This kind of bag would have been worn with either a minidress or a long ankle-length maxi-dress that was made of shiny fabric.

Black handbag with gold strap, 1970s
Leather and suede
H 81.7 cm x W 29 cm x D 4.4 cm
2006-00802

5. Tote bag with face of an Egyptian woman on the buckle, 1960s
PVC and metal
H 39.5 cm x W 38.3 cm x D 7.5 cm
Donated by Irene Hoe
2004-00653

1

2

1   Square-toed and chunky-heeled
    pumps like this pair were
    extremely popular in the
    mid 1960s. These shoes were
    usually worn with a minidress
    before calf length go-go boots
    became fashionable.

    Pumps with buckle, 1960s
    Leather and rubber
    H 10 cm x W 21 cm
    Donated by Loke Mimi
    1995-02293

2   Pumps, 1960s
    Beads, leather and rubber
    H 9.5 cm x W 21 cm
    1995-02295

3   Flat pumps with buckle, 1950s
    Suede, plastic and leather
    H 6.7 cm x W 25 cm x D 7.5 cm
    Donated by Loke Mimi
    1995-02294

4   Yellow peep-toe shoes with cut-out
    detail, Early 1970s

Leather, rubber and plastic
H 12.8 cm x W 22.7 cm x D 8 cm
Donated by Irene Hoe
2004-00668

5   White peep-toe shoes with pink
    stripes, Early 1970s
    Leather, rubber and plastic
    H 13.3 cm x Length 23 cm x D 7.9 cm
    Donated by Irene Hoe
    2004-00659

1

2

3

4

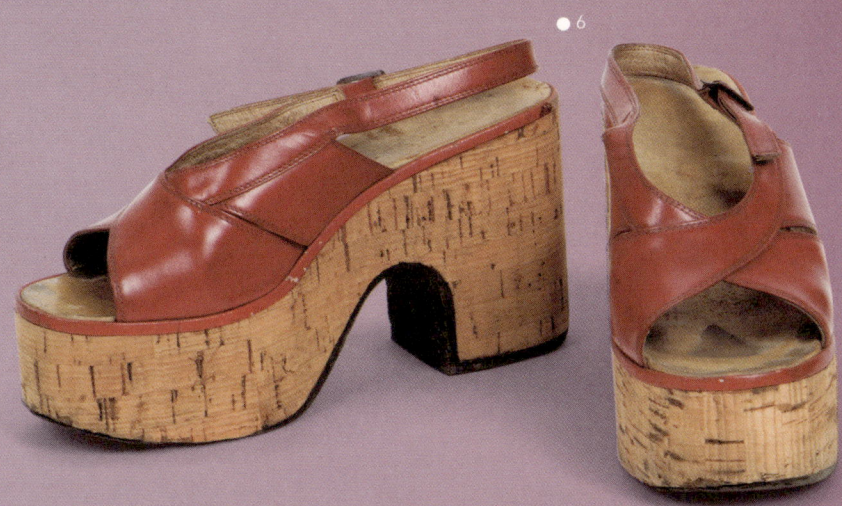

1   Slides, Mid to late 1960s
Velvet, wood, paint, beads, sequins
and leather
H 6 cm x W 23 cm
Donated by Loke Mimi
1995-02290

2   Black slides with diagonal
straps, 1970s
Leather and rubber
H 8.3 cm x W 22.1 cm x D 8.7 cm
Donated by Irene Hoe
2004-00666

3   Slides, Mid to late 1960s
Velvet, wood, water colour, sequins,
beads and leather

H 7.5 cm x W 23 cm
Donated by Loke Mimi
1995-02291

4   Slides, Mid to late 1960s
Velvet, wood, water colour, leather,
plastic and rubber
H 9 cm x W 23 cm
Donated by Loke Mimi
1995-02289

These platform shoes were extremely
popular in the early 1970s. They were
typically worn with ankle-length maxi-
dresses, miniskirts, bell-bottoms or
jeans. Shoes of this period were made
of a variety of materials such as

denim, cork and plastic, which
reflected the revolutionary period of
the 1960s and 1970s, compared to the
earlier types of wooden wedges and
leather high-heeled shoes.

5   Platform sandals, 1950s
Plastic, metal and wood
H 11 cm x W 22 cm x D 8.7 cm
Donated by Leong Wai Ying
2005-00259

6   Platform shoes, Early 1970s
Cork, leather and metal
H 12.8 cm x W 22.5 cm x D 8.2 cm
G0451

Leather and suede pumps were extremely popular among Singaporean women in the 1950s and 1960s. They were usually pointy-toed and had either a spike heel, which narrowed at the bottom, or an even narrower stiletto heel. These shoes came in various designs. In the collection, some are decorated with buckles, diamanté or bows while others are plain. One pair is made of suede printed with blue floral motifs (No. 6). Women who wanted to achieve an elongated silhouette would choose to wear these flattering shoes.

1 Pumps, Mid 1950s to early 1960s
Leather and rubber
H 15 cm x W 24.4 cm x D 7.4 cm
Donated by Irene Hoe
2004-00664

2 Pumps, Mid 1950s to early 1960s
Leather and rubber
H 14.5 cm x W 23.7 cm x D 8.2 cm
Donated by Irene Hoe
2004-00662

3 Pumps with bow,
Mid 1950s to early 1960s
Leather and rubber
H 14.5 cm x W 24.5 cm x D 7.7 cm
Donated by Irene Hoe
2004-00658

4 Pumps with diamanté buckle,
Late 1950s to early 1960s
Suede, diamanté, plastic and leather
H 14.5 cm x W 23.2 cm x D 7.6 cm
Donated by Irene Hoe
2000-00478

5 Salvatore Ferragamo black pumps,
Mid 1950s to early 1960s
Suede, satin, leather and rubber
H 15.3 cm x W 22 cm x D 7.5 cm
Donated by Irene Hoe
2004-00477

6 Pumps with printed floral motifs,
Mid 1950s to early 1960s
Suede, leather, rubber and water colour
H 12 cm x W 26 cm x D 8.6 cm
Donated by Irene Hoe
2004-00663

2

3

5

6

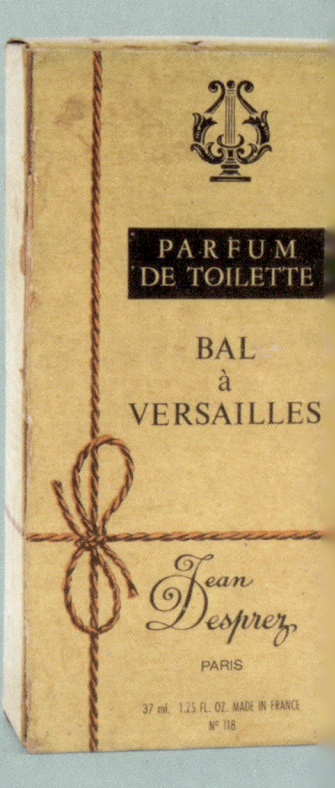

● 1   Primitif perfume by
Max Factor, 1960s
Glass, plastic and paper
H 9.7 cm x Diam. 4.2 cm
Donated by Leong Wai Ying
2005-00280

● 2   Bunga Tanjong perfume by
Fairidale, 1950s to 1960s
Glass, plastic and paper
H 10 cm x W 4.2 cm x D 4.2 cm
2001-06726

● 3   Bal à Versailles perfume by
Jean Desprey, 1960s
Glass and paper
Perfume bottle,
H 13.4 cm x W 4.4 cm x D 2.5 cm
Perfume box,
H 15.5 cm x W 7.4 cm x D 4.1 cm
Donated by Leong Wai Ying
2005-00267, 2005-00268

● 4   Charm de Molyneux Paris set of
3 perfumes with box, 1960s
Glass and paper
Perfume bottles,
H 6.3 cm x W 2.7 cm x D 1.3 cm
Box, H 7 cm x W 12 cm x D 3.9 cm
Donated by Leong Wai Ying
2005-00263, 2005-00264,
2005-00265, 2005-00266

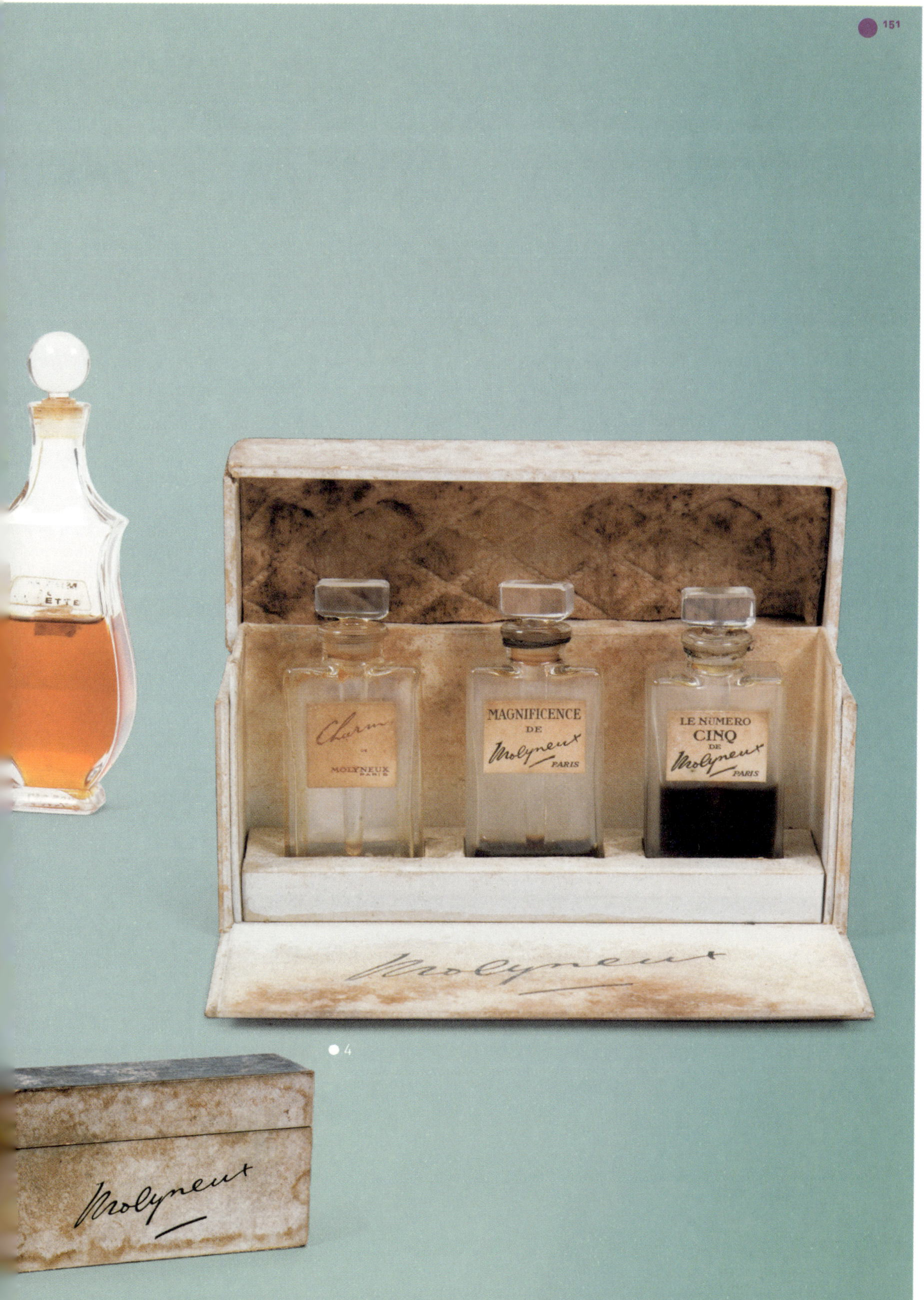
Charme
DE
MOLYNEUX
PARIS
MAGNIFICENCE
DE
Molyneux
PARIS
LE NUMERO
CINQ
DE
Molyneux
PARIS
Molyneux
Molyneux

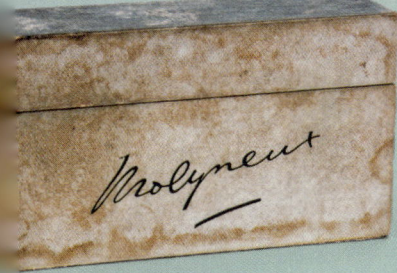

4

1   These two sterling silver perfume
bottle lids are designed in Art Deco
style, which enjoyed a revival in the
1960s. One lid has a hole for a
perfume spray mechanism.

Perfume bottles, Late 1960s
to early 1970s
Glass and sterling silver
Bottle (right), H 9 cm x Diam. 6.2 cm
Bottle (left), H 10 cm x Diam. 7 cm
Donated by Irene Hoe
2004-00669, 2004-00670

2   Perfume in a swan-shaped
holder, 1960s
Glass, metal and plastic

H 6.3 cm x W 8.2 cm x D 4 cm
Donated by Leong Wai Ying
2005-00262

3   Perfume in a shoe-shaped
holder, 1960s
Glass, metal and plastic
H 7 cm x W 8.5 cm x D 3.3 cm
Donated by Leong Wai Ying
2005-00261

4   Loose powder container with
lady-shaped lid, 1960s
Glass
H 12.7 cm x W 13.7 cm x D 10.2 cm
Donated by Leong Wai Ying
2005-00260

1

2

3

1. Butterfly brand Florida water,
1950s to 1960s
Glass, plastic, paper and aromatic
cologne containing alcohol
H 24.4 cm x Diam. 5.4 cm
2006-00388

2. Flowers brand talcum powder,
1950s to 1960s
Powder and paper
H 9.6 cm x W 4.6 cm x D 3.6 cm
2006-00387

3. Girl brand talcum powder,
1950s to 1960s
Powder and paper
H 8.5 cm x W 4 cm x D 3.5 cm
2006-00378

4. Girl brand face powder,
1950s to 1970s
Powder, plastic and paper
H 2.8 cm x W 5.3 cm x D 5.3 cm
1995-02192

5. Girl brand Florida water,
1950s to 1960s
Water, cologne, glass, plastic
and metal
H 14.8 cm x Diam. 3.5 cm
2006-00382

● 1

● 2

● 3

● 4

● 1   Max Factor lipstick, 1960s
Metal, wax and oil
H 4.5 cm x Diam. 1.9 cm
Donated by Leong Wai Ying
2005-00221

● 2   Revlon lipstick, 1960s
Metal, wax and oil
H 5.5 cm x Diam. 2 cm
Donated by Leong Wai Ying
2005-00222

● 3   Revlon lipstick with mirror, 1960s
Metal, mirror, wax and oil
H 8.1 cm x W 4 cm x Diam. 1.6 cm
Donated by Leong Wai Ying
2005-00220

● 4   Revlon lipstick, 1960s
Metal, wax and oil
H 4.9 cm x Diam. 1.5 cm
Donated by Leong Wai Ying
2005-00219

● 5   Rose face powder by Tong Hing, 1950
to 1960s
Powder and paper
Box lid,
H 5.5 cm x W 20.8 cm x D 14.2 cm
Box,
H 5.3 cm x W 20.1 cm x D 13.3 cm
Powder case lid,
H 2.3 cm x Diam. 6.3 cm
Powder case,
H 2.3 cm x Diam. 6.4 cm
2006-00389, 2006-00389-001-027

5

6

7

8

6   Soir de Paris face powder by
     Bourjois, 1960s
     Paper, plastic and powder
     H 3.8 cm x Diam. 7.6 cm
     Donated by Leong Wai Ying
     2005-00269

7   Snow White cleansing soap, 1960s
     Plastic
     H 1.2 cm x Diam. 7.7 cm
     Donated by Leong Wai Ying
     2005-00225

8   Primitif perfumed talcum powder by
     Max Factor, 1960s
     Plastic and powder
     H 13.8 cm x W 6.4 cm x D 4.4 cm
     Donated by Leong Wai Ying
     2005-00279

7

6

During the 1960s, mass-produced costume jewellery was gaining popularity around the world, including Singapore. No longer exclusively made of precious stones, jewellery became more affordable and versatile with materials like plastic, metal and diamanté. While the designs of these accessories, such as the coloured oval and round shaped clip-on earrings, are very 1960s Pop Art, the floral earrings and brooch reflect the flower-power trend, favoured by hippies in the late 1960s.

● 1 Pair of blue ear-studs, 1970s
Diamanté and metal
H 1.4 cm x Diam. 2.4 cm
Donated by Nalini C. Chentilly
2005-01256

● 2 Fan-shaped earrings with matching brooch, 1960s

Metal
Earrings, H 0.5–0.7 cm x W 3.1 cm
Brooch H 2–3.7 cm x W 6.4 cm
Donated by Leong Wai Ying
2005-00213, 2005-00214

● 3 Set of rose earrings with matching necklace, 1960s
Ivory and metal
Earrings,
H 2.2 cm x W 2.2 cm x D 2 cm
Necklace,
H 1.4 cm x W 12 cm x D 14 cm
Donated by Nancy Lim
2005-01195, 2005-01196

● 4 Heart-shaped jewellery box, 1960s
Metal and velvet
H 5.2 cm x W 9.4 cm x D 7.7 cm
Donated by Leong Wai Ying
2005-00258

● 5 Pair of flame-like clip-on earrings,
Late 1950s
Diamanté and metal
H 5.8 cm x W 3 cm x D 1.5 cm
Donated by Nancy Lim
2005-01194

● 6 Pair of pearl studs, 1970s
Metal and pearl
H 1.7 cm x Diam. 2.3 cm
Donated by Nalini C. Chentilly
2005-01255

● 7 Plastic earrings and floral brooch,
Late 1960s to early 1970s
Plastic and metal
H 1–2.6 cm x Diam. 2–7 cm
Donated by Leong Wai Ying
2005-00232, 2005-00233, 2005-00234,
2005-00235, 2005-00236, 2005-00208,
2005-00209, 2005-00210, 2005-00211,
2005-00206, 2005-00207

1   Black eyewear, 1950s
Plastic, glass and metal
H 4 cm x W 15.5 cm x D 14.4 cm
Donated by Low Suet Hing
2005-00361

2   Black eyewear, 1950s to 1960s
Plastic, glass and metal
H 4.1 cm x W 15.5 cm x D 13.7 cm
2005-01175

3   In the 1950s, butterfly spectacles or cat's-eye frames were very popular among women in Singapore. The lenses were straight on top and round below, and the corner of the frames tilted upwards. These two pairs of frames are similar in design. While the black and ivory-layered pair has winged corners, the brown and white-layered pair feature a half rim. These glasses were usually decorated or engraved with designs or rhinestones.

Black and brown layered cat's-eye frames, 1950s
Plastic, glass and metal
H 4.5 cm x W 14.1–14.5 cm x D 12–12.3 cm
2005-01174, 2005-01176

4   Hair curlers and pins, 1960s
Plastic and sponge
H 3.5 cm x W 6.3 cm x D 3.5 cm
Donated by Leong Wai Ying
2005-00239, 2005-00043, 2005-
00244, 2005-00248, 2005-00249,
2005-00250, 2005-00251

5   Mirror, 1960s
Glass, plastic and paper
H 19.2 cm x W 18.4 cm
2006-00375

● 1

● 2

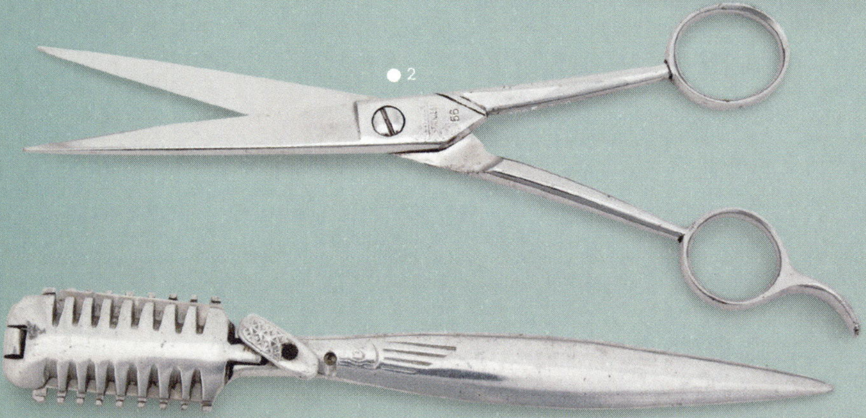

● 1 Hairbrush and mirror set, Late
1960s to early 1970s
Nylon and sterling silver
Mirror,
H 29 cm x W 10.2 cm x D 1 cm
Hairbrush,
H 3.8 cm x W 25 cm x D 8.5 cm
Donated by Irene Hoe
2004-00671, 2004-00672

● 2 Scissors and shaver set,
1950s to 1960s
Steel
Scissors,
H 19.5 cm W x 5.2 cm x D 0.9 cm
Shaver,
H 18.2 cm x W 2.7 cm x D 1.3 cm
2005-00237, 2005-00238

● 3 Hair clips, 1960s
Metal and paper
H 13.1 cm x W 9 cm
2006-00390

● 4 Glo Co liquid hairdressing oil, 1950s
Glass, oil, metal and paper
H 16.5 cm x Diam. 5.5 cm
Donated by Oh Beng Swee
2004-00088

● 5 Lavender Solidified Brilliantine hair
cream by Yardley, 1930s to 1950s
Tin, wax and oil
H 2.4 cm x Diam. 8.3 cm
1995-02659

● 6 Lavender solidified brilliantine hair
cream by Yardley, 1950s to 1960s
Metal, wax, oil, paper and glass
H 5 cm x Diam. 5 cm
1995-02660

● 7 Bulah Terang Minyak Rambut
Krinting hair oil, 1960s
Glass, oil, metal and paper
H 14.7 cm x W 5 cm x D 3.3 cm
2000-08206

● 3

4

Glo-Co
LIQUID HAIR DRESSING
KEEPS THE HAIR WELL GROOMED
AND GIVES A NATURAL LUSTRE
GLO-CO COMPANY
LOS ANGELES   CALIFORNIA

5

LAVENDER
SOLIDIFIED
BRILLIANTINE
YARDLEY
LONDON
ENGLAND

6

YARDLEY
Lavender
SOLIDIFIED
BRILLIANTINE
70 G.

7

BULAN TERANG
MINYAK
RAMBUT KRINTING

● 1

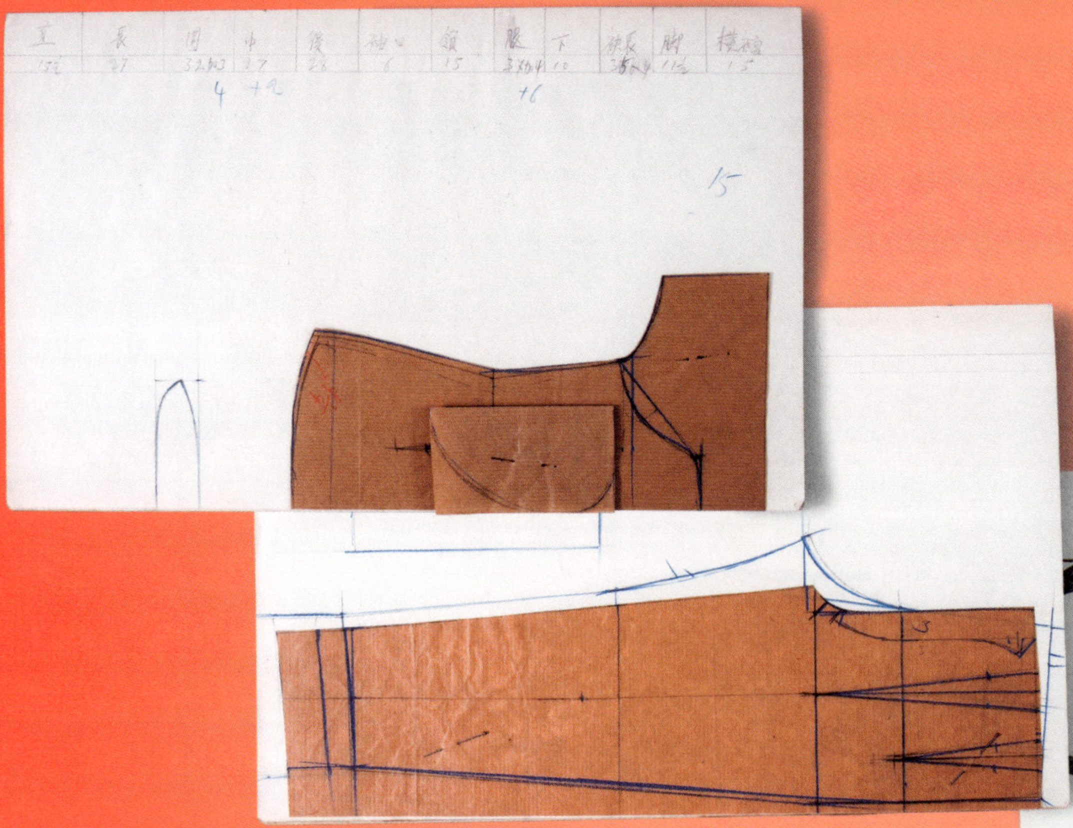

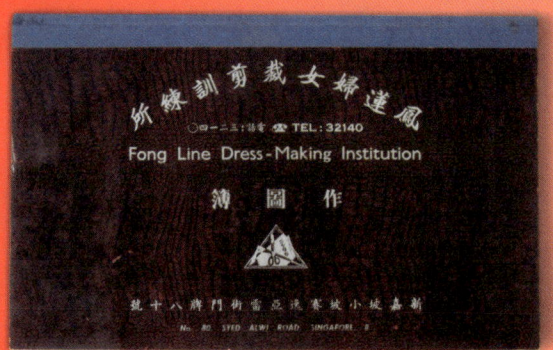

工	長	圍	中	後	袖口	領	腰	下	袖長	腳	橫檔
42	37	32ⁿ3	37	2½	6	15	3×4+4 10	佳 14	1½	1.5	

4 +2   +6

15

祈練訓剪裁女婦蓮鳳
○四一二三:話電 ☎ TEL : 32140
Fong Line Dress-Making Institution
簿 圖 作
號十八 街門 當 店 洪 寨 坡 小 嘉 新
No. 80 IFED ALWI ROAD SINGAPORE 8

● 1   This dressmaking book contains notes and paper patterns of several garments such as the traditional *cheongsam*, or men's shirts and trouser suits. Students were usually asked to make clothes in miniature sizes with sample patterns such as those found in this dressmaking book. In the 1950s and 1960s, it was not unusual for women in Singapore to pick up sewing skills from Community Centres and private commercial schools. Mass production of clothes in Singapore only became widespread in the 1970s.

Dressmaking book, 1960s
Paper
H 38.6 cm x W 24.8 cm
Donated by Mak Wai Har
1995-00682

● 2   Sewing book, 1950s–1960s
Paper
H 21.1 cm x W 15.1 cm
Donated by Mak Wai Har
1995-00680

An Indian Print Street Wear

Fabric required : 90cm. × 5 m

How to sew- Stitch darts in front, back bodice. Interface front bodice with silk organdy. Make buttonholes. Join front and back at shoulders. Sew back collar to neck-edge of bodice. Join collar with facing and cover interfacing at edge. Feather-stitch 2 **places** to hold. Seam sides and leave side free for opening. Join seam of sleeve and hand roll sleeve edge. Gather upper edges of sleeve. Fold tucks on front and back skirts. Stitch darts. Leave side for opening free and seam sides. Join waist and insert zipper. Hem. Sew sleeve into armhole. Sew on buttons.

A Vermilion Colored Suit for Juniors

Fabric required : 90cm. × 3.5m

How to sew- Stitch darts in skirt, bodice and sleeve. Make button hole. Sew slash opening in skirt, front, back bodice and sleeve. Sew skirt waist lining, seam sides. Insert zipper, facing and stitch from right side 2cm. from edge. Sew neck facing and front facing. Join sleeve to armhole and finish hem. Stitch neckline and hem 3cm from edge. Sew vinyl leather vestee and bind edge with vermilion colored fabric. Sew snap on vestee and bodice to hold.

H. on page 7

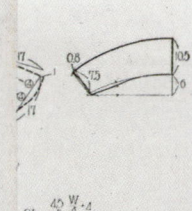

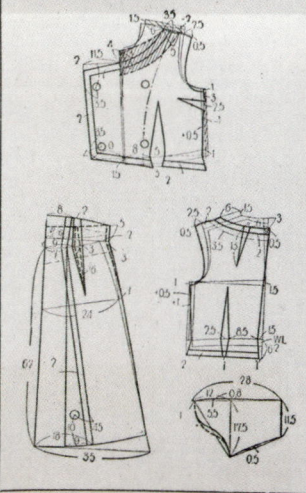

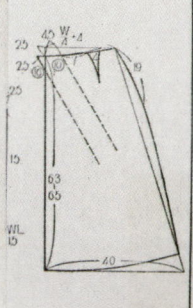

HOW TO SEW 6 DRESSES

by Enko Fujikawa

WOMEN'S STANDARD DRESS MEASUREMENT

Description	Large	Med-ium	Small	How to measure
Neck	37	36	35	measure around neck
Shoulder width	37	36	35	measure from left to right shoulder from back
Back waist length	39.5	38	36.5	Measure from "bump" at back of neck to waist
Dress length	* 31 141	* 30 136	* 29 133	measure back waist length and down to floor *
Chest width	34	33	32	measure from center of armhole seam across the chest
Back width	35	34	33	measure from seam at middle of back straight across to armhole seam
Bust	19.5 88	19 84	18 82	
Waist	68	64	60	measure around the natural waist line rather tightly
Hip	71 96	20 92	19 88	measure around fullest part of hip
Sleeve length	52	55	52	measure from seam of armhole to wrist, loosely
Arm band	30	28	27	measure loosely around the fullest part of arm
Elbow band	25	23	22	measure loosely around elbow
Wrist band	16.5	16	15.5	measure around wrist
Width of hand	21	20	19.5	Bend thumb clasp with other four fingers and measure

* Cuban heel is worn, when measuring from floor.
‡ From waist to hip.

CHILDREN'S STANDARD DRESS MEASUREMENT

Description \ Age	1	3	5	7	9	11	13
Neck	26.2	27.5	28.8	30.1	31.4	32.7	34
Width of back shoulders	23.2	25	26.8	28.6	30.4	32.2	34
Back length	20	22.5	25	27.5	30	32.5	35
Bust	64	70	74	76	80	84	88
Waist		54	55	56.5	58	60	62
Hip	66	70	74	76	80	84	88
Dress length	25 33	40	48	57	66	75	84
Sleeve length	23	27.5	32	36.5	41	45.5	50
Arm band	18	19.5	21	22.5	24	25.5	27
Width of Hand	15.2	16	16.8	17.6	18.4	19.2	20
Length of short pants	25	27	30	34	38	48	‡
Length of long pants	42	50	58	66	74	82	90
Inseam measurement	21	22	23	24	25.5	26	27.5

* According to age, 15 to 10cm of ease is added to Bust and Hip.
‡ Unit / cm

SINGAPORE HOME

Living in newly built and affordable homes, few could deny their standard of living had risen dramatically. Aspirations surged and the collection reflects this golden age.

Today, Singapore can be considered a house-proud nation. A love of home upgrading, the success of home-furnishing stores such as IKEA and the purchase of new furnishings every Hari Raya, Deepavali or Chinese New Year are all evidence of this.

Before the 1960s, however, most Singaporeans lived in poor conditions. Squalid shop houses, many of which had no modern sanitation, were crammed with several families who were at the mercy of landlords. Other families lived in ramshackle *attap* (palm leaf) huts and zinc-roofed houses.

In outlying areas, people squatted on vacant land or lived in well-organised *kampongs* (villages). *Kampong* living was more spacious than shop house living, but even there, conditions were not free of hardship.

As there was no running water, some families depended on wells for their drinking water and for washing. However, not all *kampongs* had the

In recent years, shop houses have become highly desirable homes. During the 1950s, however, squalid conditions meant the opposite.

convenience of a well or a pond, and many villagers had to rely on public standpipes for their water supply. Like the shop house dwellers, villagers lived with no modern sanitation and had to rely upon night-soil collection.

Despite the rudimentary housing, there was still an appealing side to *kampong* life. Residents possessed a fierce sense of loyalty, and the communal spirit meant villagers would take care of each other's families and property. Whenever disagreements arose, they would be settled by the *kampong* chief. In some *kampongs*, villagers of different races lived close together and even shared meals together.

As the post-World-War-II population boomed, the colonial government recognised the need to boost housing supply. The Singapore Improvement Trust had been set up in 1927, but its original purpose was not to build housing for the masses. It was only after World War II that the Trust attempted the clearing of slums and the construction of public housing on a larger scale. However, these efforts alleviated the

Singapore's burgeoning population meant an increased demand for housing. From the late 1950s, families were gradually relocated away from crowded shop houses or *kampong*s into new flats.

The new HDB flats provided plenty of space in which to enjoy all the new amenities of the era.

housing shortage only slightly. It was only when the Housing & Development Board (HDB) was formed in 1960, after Singapore had attained self-government, that real progress began.

By 1966, a quarter of all households had been moved into HDB flats. With the HDB's massive building and resettlement programme, this figure would increase to a third by 1970 and two-thirds by 1980. Of these, the vast majority would own the flat they lived in, thanks to public subsidies and the use of Central Provident Fund savings.

As standards of living rose, so did aspirations. By 1966, 80 per cent of households had electricity, and it was natural they would desire the modern conveniences of the late twentieth century.

With its affordable $5 monthly subscription and local programming, the Rediffusion cable radio set was soon found in almost every home. In the 1960s, it was part of daily family life and it was not uncommon for homes to have their radio switched on from morning to night. The popularity of Rediffusion—and radio in general—would eventually be eroded by television, which made its advent in 1963.

Television generated a lot of excitement but at first it was generally considered a luxury. Aside from the daunting price tag, it may not have

seemed worthwhile to purchase a set because
of the paucity of programming—in April 1963,
Channel 5 was broadcasting only five hours of
English and Malay programmes on weekdays and
ten hours on weekends. Chinese and Tamil
broadcasts commenced only later that year, on
Channel 8. Colour broadcasts began in 1974, and by
1977, more than 300,000 households owned a
television set. The museum's collection includes
brightly coloured Philips and Teleton television sets
that were popular in the 1970s.

Plastic furnishings were particularly sought
after. This trend can be credited to the surge in
Italian designers who brought new meaning to
plastic, transforming its reputation from cheap to
desirable. During the 1960s, the Scandinavians and
the Italians spearheaded the evolution of colourful
and creatively shaped plastic furniture. Even
mundane appliances such as the standard desk
telephone were recreated in the 1960s using
brightly-coloured plastic.

With the influx of entertainment and modern
conveniences, the concept of home changed from
being a place families used for essential aspects of
daily life—such as sleeping, eating and cleaning—to
a place where they would choose to spend their
leisure hours as well.

This page from top: HDB flats being built in 1965; a balloting of flats ceremony at an HDB estate in 1965, where prospective tenants waited to hear names of the successful applicants being called.

Opposite from top: A typical modern kitchen of the 1950s; home furnishings displayed at the John Little department store; Television Singapura, Singapore's first television station, was launched in February 1963. Regular transmission started two months later.

the quality
is remembered
long after
the price
is forgotten

● 4

● 5

Tiffin carriers were a common sight in Singapore in the 1950s and 1960s. 'Tiffin' is a word of Anglo-Indian origin meaning a light meal of curry or lunch. Tiffin carriers were used to carry food from the home to work, or for food bought from food vendors. These 1960s ornate tiffin carriers were imported from Czechoslovakia, while others were manufactured locally. Ornate enamelled tiffin carriers were commonly used by the Peranakan Chinese for picnics.

1

2

3

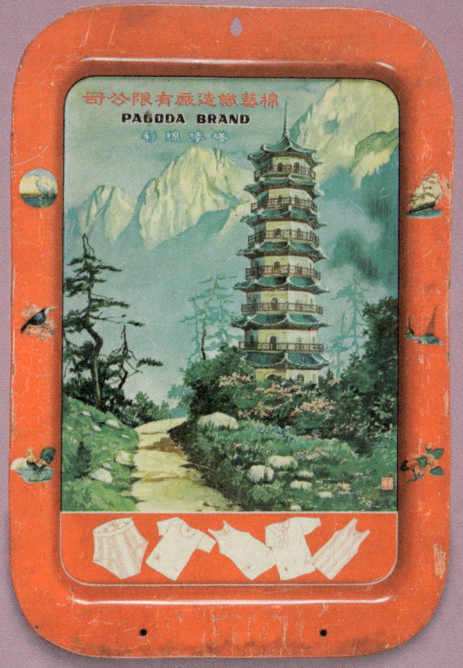

1 Ray O Vac flashlight batteries
   advertising signboard, 1950s
   Metal
   H 60.5 cm x W 35.5 cm
   2000-03650

2 Swallow brand rubber sandals
   advertising signboard, 1970s
   Metal
   H 44.3 cm x W 74.9 cm
   2000-03548

3 Jintan toothpaste advertising
   signboard, 1950s
   Metal
   H 60 cm x W 35.5 cm
   2000-03650

4 Pagoda Brand advertisement
   tray, Singapore, 1950s to 1960s
   Metal
   H 38.5 cm x W 25.5 cm x D 1.4 cm
   2000-03594

5 Axe Brand Oil by Leong Kai Fook
   advertisement tray featuring a
   pagoda, Singapore, 1950s
   Metal
   Diam. 32.7 cm x D 1.5 cm
   2000-03619

6 Wong Yiu Nam Medical Hall
   paper bag, 1960s
   Paper and nylon
   H 29 cm x W 43.5 cm x D 17 cm
   1995-05002

1 Alladin Lamp, 1970s
Wood and canvas
H 148 cm x D 37 cm
2006-00506

2 Toshiba toaster, 1970s
Metal and plastic
H 25 cm x W 28 cm x D 14.5 cm
2006-00501

3 Orange Siemens iron, 1970
Metal and plastic
H 10 cm x W 22.5 cm x D 11 cm
2006-00591

4 Sunflower breakfast set milk
container, 1970s
Glass
H 12.5 cm x W 21.5 cm x D 13.5 cm
2006-00537

5 Sunflower breakfast set jug, 1970
Glass
H 18.5 cm x W 17.5 cm x D 10 cm
2006-00536-001

6 Sunflower breakfast set coffee
mug, 1970s
Glass
H 7.5 cm x W 8.5 cm x D 7 cm
2006-00526

7 Orange pot, 1970s
Enamel
H 11.5 cm x W 25 cm x D 18 cm
2006-00594-001

4

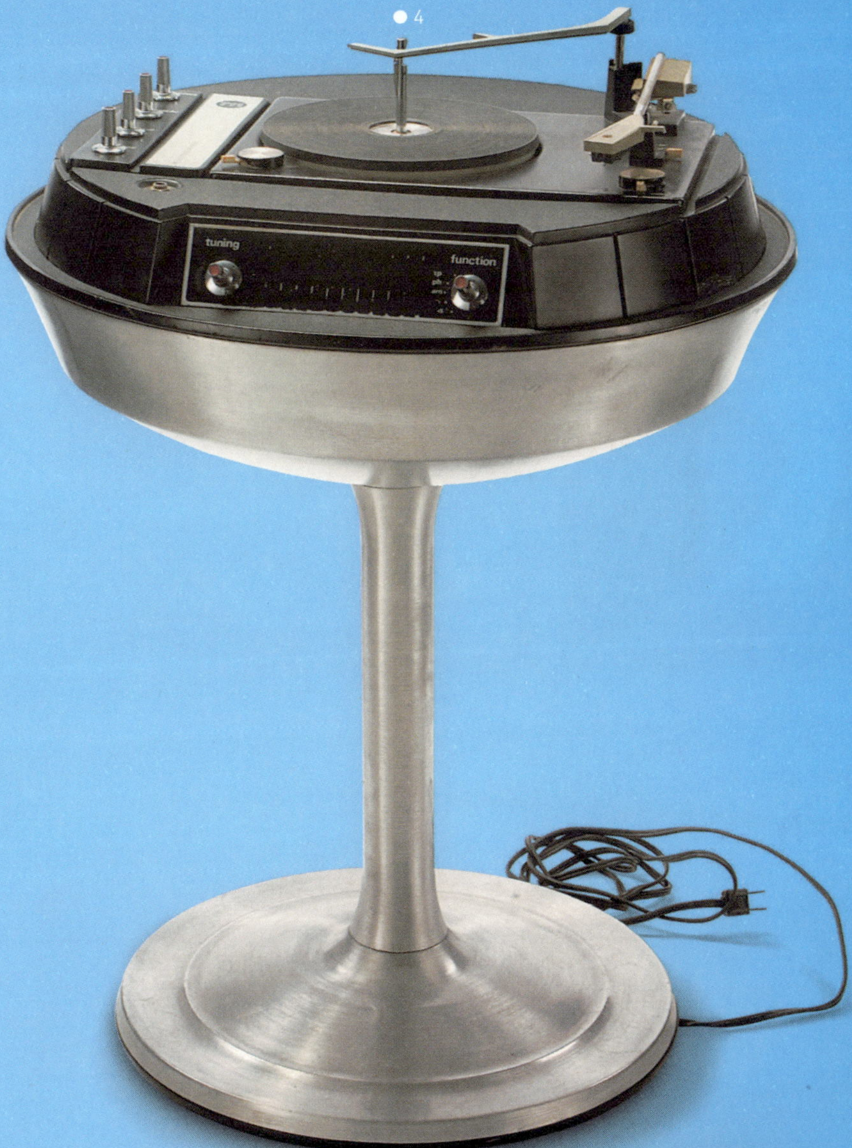

tuning function

5

1 Philips Discovery Helmet
television, 1970s
Metal and plastic
H 41 cm x W 52 cm x D 53 cm
2006-00507

2 Silver radio, 1970s
Metal
H 24.1 cm x W 34 cm x D 11.7 cm
2006-00224

3 Telefunken digital radio, 1970s
Metal
H 9.5 cm x W 33.5 cm x D 16 cm
2006-00523

4 Spacegram, 1970s
Metal and plastic
H 81 cm x D 52 cm
2006-00497

5 Speakers for spacegram, 1970s
Metal
H 19 cm x W 19 cm x D 18 cm
2006-00497.004-5

1 Pifco hairdryer with box, 1950s
Plastic, metal and rubber
H 10.8 cm x W 22.7 cm x D 27.8 cm
2006-01228

2 Handy Hannah hairdryer, 1950s
Plastic and metal
H 31.3 cm x W 18.1 cm x D13.2 cm
Cord with plug, L 160 cm
2006-01227

3 Wahl Silent hairdryer, 1960s
Plastic, metal and rubber
H 10.4 cm x W 30.3 cm x D 20.2 cm
2006-01229

4 Telephone stand, Singapore, 1970,
Mixed material
H 62 cm x W 85 cm x D 33 cm
2006-00499

5 Orange telephone, 1970s
Plastic and metal
H 12 cm x W 24 cm x D 20 cm
2006-00502

● Picture Credits

The publisher would like to thank the following for permission to reproduce their photographs:

Angelo Cavalli/Zefa/Corbis, 192

Annie Teo, 99 (top and below), 136 (top)

David Zaitz/Photonica Inc/Photolibrary, 90–91

Frederick William York courtesy of the National Archives of Singapore, 22 (centre)

Freitag/Zefa/Corbis, 186–187

Gregor Schuster/zefa/Corbis, 2

Hawker AJ courtesy of the National Archives of Singapore, 60 (centre and below)

John Pratt/Hulton Archive/Getty Images, 5

John Randall courtesy of the National Archives of Singapore, 55

KF Wong courtesy of the National Archives of Singapore, 13, 14–15, 23 (top), 52, 54, 57, 60, 99 (centre), 132–133

Lim Kheng Chye's Collection at the National Archives of Singapore, 30

Ministry of Information, Communication and the Arts courtesy of the National Archives of Singapore, 10, 11, 17, 18, 20, 23 (below), 26, 32, 33, 34 (below), 58, 92, 96, 98 (below), 130, 135, 136 (centre and below), 137 (top), 168, 170, 171, 174 (below), 175 (centre and below)

National Archives of Singapore, 8, 21, 22 (top), 22 (below), 23 (centre), 28, 34 (top), 35 (top and below), 56, 97, 98 (centre), 137 (centre and below), 174 (top)

National Museum of Singapore, 34 (centre), 98 (top)

Pete Starman/Photonica/alt.Type Images, 24–25

Public Works Department courtesy of the National Archives of Singapore, 187 (top)

Ruediger Knobloch/A.B./Zefa/Corbis, 132–133

Stacy Morrison/Zefa/Corbis, 178–179

Thomas Kennett courtesy of the National Museum of Singapore, 29

Wendy Hitchell-Jones (nee) Wendy Toh Kim Kee courtesy of the National Museum of Singapore, 94–95

Wong Kwan courtesy of the National Archives of Singapore, 35 (centre), 61 (top), 172, 173

● Bibliography

Ahmad Sarji. *P. Ramlee: Erti Yang Sakti*. Subang Jaya. Malaysia: Pelanduk Publications (M) Sdn Bhd, 1999.

Auge International. *Singapore: A Decade of Progress*. Singapore: Auge International, 1975.

Barnard, Timothy P. "Vampires, Heroes and Jesters: A History of Cathay Keris." In *The Cathay Story*, edited by Wong Ain-ling. Hong Kong: Hong Kong Film Archive, 2002.

Chan Kwok Bun & Tong Chee Kiong. *Past Times: A Social History of Singapore*. Singapore: Times Editions, 2003.

Chew, Ernest and Edwin Lee. *A History of Singapore*. Singapore: Oxford University Press, 1991.

Chia, Josephine. *Frog under a Coconut Shell*. Singapore: Times Books International, 2002.

Chin, Audrey and Constance Singam. *Singapore Women Re-Presented*. Singapore: Landmark Books, 2004.

Chua, Beng Huat (1995) "That Imagined Space: Nostalgia for the Kampung in Singapore." *In Portraits of Places: History, Community and Identity in Singapore*. Edited by Barbara S.A. Yeoh and Lily Kong. Singapore: Times Editions, 1995.

Chua, Beng Huat. "Hybridity, Ethnicity and Food in Singapore." In *Life Is Not Complete Without Shopping: Consumption Culture in Singapore*. Singapore: Singapore University Press, 2003.

Chua, Beng Huat. *Fashion Shopping: Programs, Stages and Audience*. Department of Sociology Working Papers, No. 102, National University of Singapore: 1990.

Garner, Philippe. *Sixties Design*. London: Taschen, 2003.

Goh Chor Boon. *Serving Singapore: A Hundred Years of Cold Storage 1903-2003*. Singapore: Cold Storage Singapore, 2003.

Gopalakrishnan, V. and Ananda Perera. *Singapore Changing Landscapes: Geylang, Chinatown, Serangoon*. Singapore: FEP International, 1983.

Handley, Susannah. *Nylon, the Manmade Fashion Revolution: A Celebration of Design from Art Silk to Nylon and Thinking Fibres*. London: Bloomsbury, 1999.

Harding, James and Ahmad Sarji. *P. Ramlee: The Bright Star*. Subang Jaya, Malaysia: Pelanduk Publications (M) Sdn Bhd, 2002.

Hiltebeitel, Alf and Barbara D. Miller ed. *Hair: Its Power and Meaning in Asian Cultures*. Albany: State University of New York Press, 1998.

Jamil Sulong. *Kaca Permata: Memoir Seorang Pengarah*. Kuala Lumpur: Dewan Bahasa and Pustaka Kementrian Pendidikan, 1990.

Kong, Lily and T.C. Chang. *Joo Chiat: A Living Legacy*. Singapore: Editions Didier Millet, 2001.

Kras, Reyer. *Icons of Design: The 20th Century*. Munich, New York: Prestel, 2000.

Lee Choo Neo. *The Life of a Chinese Girl in Singapore*. Singapore, 1913.

Lee, Chin Koon and Shermay Lee. *Mrs Lee's Cookbook*. Singapore: Eurasia Press, 2003.

Lee, Chor Lin. *Batik: Creating an Identity*. Singapore: National Museum, 1991.

Lim, Kay Tong. *Cathay—55 Years of Cinema*. Singapore: Landmark Books, 1991.

Lipinski, Kathie and Bob Lipinski. *The Complete Beverage Dictionary, 2nd Edition*. New York: Van Nostrand Reinhold, 1999.

Liu, Gretchen. *Singapore: A Pictorial History 1819-2000*. Singapore: Editions Didier Millet in association with the National Heritage Board, 1999.

Ministry of Culture. *Singapore Facts and Pictures*. Singapore: Ministry of Culture, 1978.

Ministry of National Development and the Economic Research Centre. *Singapore Sample Household Survey, 1966*. Singapore: The University of Singapore, 1966.

National Heritage Board and Fashion Designers Society. *Costumes through Time: Singapore*. Singapore: National Heritage Board and Fashion Designers Society, 1993.

Chan Kwee Sung. *One More Story to Tell: Memories of Singapore 1930s-1980s*. Singapore: Landmark Books, 2005.

Opie, Robert. *Remember When: A Nostalgic Trip through the Consumer Era*. London: Octopus Publishing Group, 1999.

Quah, Stella. *Family in Singapore: Sociological Perspectives*. Singapore: Times Academic Press, 1998.

Report of the Singapore Housing Committee, 1947. Singapore: Government Printing Office, 1948.

Schiffer, Nancy. *The Best of Costume Jewelry, revised edition with value guide*. Lancaster, PA: Schiffer Publishing Ltd., 1996.

Shaw Organisation. *The Shaw Story*. www.shaw.com.sg/shawstory/shawstory.htm, 2001.

Department of Statistics. *Singapore, 1965-1995 Statistical Highlights, A Review of 30 Years' Development*. Singapore: Department of Statistics, 1995.

Singapore: The Encyclopedia. Singapore: Editions Didier Millet and the National Heritage Board 2006.

Smith, Andrew F (Ed.). *The Oxford Encyclopedia of Food and Drink in America Volume 1*. Oxford: Oxford University Press, 2004.

Smith, Desire. *Fashion Footwear: 1800-1970 A Schiffer Book for Collectors*. Lancaster, PA: Schiffer Publishing, 2000.

Sommar, Ingrid. *Scandinavian Style: Classic and Modern*. London: Carlton, 2003.

Steele, Valerie and Laird Borrelli. *Bags: A Lexicon of Style*. London: Scriptum Editions, 2006.

Steele, Valerie. *Fifty Years of Fashion : New Look to Now*. New Haven, CT: Yale University Press, 1997.

Tambini, Michael. *The Look of the Century: Design Icons of the 20th Century*. London; Dorling Kindersley, 1999.

Tan, Sylvia. *Singapore Heritage Food: Yesterday's Recipes for Today's Cooks*. Singapore: Landmark Books, 2004.

Turnbull, C.M. *A History of Singapore, 1819-1988*. Singapore: Oxford University Press, 1989.

Uhde, Jan and Yvonne Ng Udhe. *Latent Images: Film in Singapore*. Singapore: Oxford University Press, 2000.

Van der Heide, William. *Malaysian Cinema, Asian Film Border Crossings and National Culture*. Armsterdam: University of Armsterdam Press, 2002.